"In the tradition of *Good to Great*, *The Navigator's Handbook* is a people-based, action-oriented, practical guide designed to bring out the best in your leadership abilities. David's wonderful sense of narrative and pace provides insights through passed-along wisdom from some surprising sources. *The Navigator's Handbook* helps you chart your own course to personal discovery and leadership excellence."

—DOUGLAS A. BOWEN
President and CEO, PeoplesBank

"David O'Brien recognizes how critical behaviors and our desire for a higher purpose in an organization and in our lives can define success or failure for a company, a team, and a person. He captures a lifetime of developing winning teams and people and puts them in simple, easy-to-follow lessons for managers at all levels that will lead to the Navigator's path. It is well worth reading."

—ARTHUR BANKS
Chief Operating Officer (Retired),
Blue Cross Blue Shield of Massachusetts

"David's style is welcoming and draws you in to the conversation. By sharing hi .... know this is not a prescriptive .... through it, David becom stunning vistas as well as ble spots along the leaɑ lessons learned allow for the reader to start to cᴏɴꜱᴛʀᴜᴄt their own experiences and go back for reinforcement, reminders, and renewal whenever needed."

—DEEPIKA NATH, PH.D.

Founder & Principal, Indica Consulting

"*The Navigator's Handbook* is an excellent primer for anyone who is, or wants to become, a highly successful leader. Using real-life examples and his personal experiences, David O'Brien provides lots of practical advice and shows you how to become a true leader—in business and in life."

—BRUCE BEATT

General Counsel and Secretary, The Stanley Works

"*The Navigator's Handbook* offers an inspiring and fresh framework for leadership. The lessons and exercises provide a clear path for bringing out the best in ourselves and our employees. The author reminds us that leadership is both an intellectual and emotional calling, worthy of our highest effort."

—LINDA TODARO

Chief Administrative Officer, RiverBend Medical Group

"*The Navigator's Handbook* is an adventure in leadership learning that should grace every manager's credenza. Author David O'Brien uses a conversational tone to engage the reader in a tutorial about work-place behaviors, which successful leaders must recognize and effectively manage. The journey is rich with practical advice on how to help transform challenging team members into navigators—who appreciate the opportunity to enhance their careers and invest in their company's success. The lessons in *The Navigator's Handbook* make leadership development a joyful experience. This book will improve your relationships with your team members and everyone in your life."

—JAMES MATHEWSON
Editor in Chief, ibm.com

"Inspirational, practical, and clear. Complete with instructions, exercises, lessons, and examples, *The Navigator's Handbook* is a must read for anyone who wants to grow as a respected and inspired leader. David's writing style is refreshing and engaging."

—HOLLY COHEN
Career Coach

"*The Navigator's Handbook* reflects the practicality of David O'Brien's understanding of the impact of personal values on the inherent truth that great leadership is within the reach of us all once we know ourselves and are willing to inspect how we live our personal and professional lives. *The Navigator's Handbook* provides the tools and the inspirational impetus for the introspection necessary to maximize the God-given talents we all possess and need to nurture. *The Navigator's Handbook* is both a mirror providing an opportunity for reflection and a guidepost by which to take measure of our leadership impact and growth. For those interested in developing their leadership qualities, *The Navigator's Handbook* is a must read."

—JOHN HONOR
Executive Director, Human Resources,
Global Professional Services Organization

THE
NAVIGATOR'S
HANDBOOK

★

To:

Bernice
Mariqueo,

Choose
to.
Navigate!

David O'Brien

THE
NAVIGATOR'S
HANDBOOK

101 LEADERSHIP LESSONS

for WORK *and* LIFE

Third Edition

DAVID A. O'BRIEN

**PURPOSE
DRIVEN
PUBLISHING**

PURPOSE
DRIVEN
PUBLISHING

Purpose Driven Publishing
141 Weston Street, #155
Hartford, CT, 06141

The opinions expressed by the Author are not necessarily those held by Purpose Driven Publishing.

Ordering Information: Quantity sales and special discounts are available on quantity purchases by corporations, associations, and others. For details, contact the publisher at the address above.

Cover & Interior Design by Leah LeFlore
Printed in the United States of America.
ISBN-10: 1-946384-08-9
ISBN-13: 978-1-946384-08-9
Library of Congress Control Number: 2017938666

The information contained within this book is strictly for informational purposes. The material may include information, products, or services by third parties. As such, the Author and Publisher do not assume responsibility or liability for any third party material or opinions. Readers are advised to do their own due diligence when it comes to making decisions.

Purpose Driven Publishing works with authors, and aspiring authors, who have a story to tell and a brand to build. Do you have a book idea you would like us to consider publishing? Please visit www.purposedrivenpublishing.com for more information.

D E D I C A T I O N

To my father, whose life was a master class in Navigating.
Happy Birthday, Dad

A C K N O W L E D G E M E N T S

To Gabriela:
Thank you for your daily lessons and inspiration.
Oh the places you will go!

To Constanza:
Thank you for believing and for the many lessons along the way.

To Catherine and Deepika:
Thank you for your encouragement.

To all my friends and colleagues who continue to inspire me:
Thank you!

To My Dear Mother:
Thank you for your love, prayers, and inspiration.

TABLE *of* CONTENTS

"If we would only give, just once, the same amount of
time and reflection to what we want to get out of life
as we do to the question of what to do with two weeks
vacation, we would be startled at our false standards
and the aimless procession of our busy days."

—Dorothy Canfield-Fisher
American Author & Essayist
1879–1958

THE GIFT *of* DISCOVERY

Like many of my colleagues in the early 1980s, I was thrust into the management ranks almost by default. The company needed a leader and I was next in line for a promotion. A dear mentor once told me I had "all the fuel you'll need on your journey to success"—hard work, commitment, fair play, sacrifice, etc. But I wasn't always successful in using these ingredients for the best of the organization or myself. I found myself running faster and faster while losing sight of the bigger picture, all the while losing ground in some small, yet-to-be discovered way. Before I became aware of the insights laid out in this book, I struggled to come to terms with the many different styles, work ethics, dreams, fears, and expectations of the people I was chosen to lead. But I knew that all of the elements in this boiling sea of change were in some way linked to the challenge of leadership. As time went on and I gained leadership experience, I began to make my way through the sea of change with effectiveness and grace. Still, my understanding of the defining elements to leadership success was fragmentary. I had yet to put all the complex currents of leadership into a cohesive system.

I needed to step back from the day-to-day challenges of management to get a clear picture of what distinguished good leadership from bad. The formula began to come together while I was on a much-needed sabbatical. At first I was at sea without a compass. I wasn't sure what all of the material presented here meant. But I was sure that the observations and reflections of the past several years had produced more truths about life and leadership than I had discovered in the previous twenty years of working in corporate America. Slowly through months of deep thought, I found my compass and navigated my way to an understanding of all these truths. In a way, the title of this book reflects my own process of discovery as well as my hope that readers of this book will find their own way too.

At first, the thread of discovery woven throughout the fabric of reflection encompassed leadership and all of its many obstacles. Sure, I had read dozens of related books and attended more than my fair share of seminars. But somehow, I was still not entirely convinced that I had found the set of traits that allow leaders at any level to thrive and prosper despite the endless array of storms and mines along the way. In addition to tapping the many formal lessons of my leadership career, I chose to look beyond these lessons to a place where I believe great leadership lies dormant in many of us—the heart. As I began to tap this amazing source of universal wisdom, I came to realize that so many of my great leadership colleagues shared a set of qualities or characteristics that made good leadership look easy, almost effortless. As I began to unravel this mystery, I discovered that these qualities had a central theme—these great leaders operated with a sense of clarity and higher purpose that allowed them to successfully lead their people through the toughest storms of organizational change and transformation.

I also discovered that this sense of clarity and higher

purpose transcended the workplace to a point where they seemed to navigate other areas of life successfully as well. This acknowledgement led me to believe that I was much closer to the true leadership formula than I had expected. It also served as a powerful guidepost and inspiration for the title of this book. Time and time again, these great leaders beat the odds and turned everyday leadership obstacles into opportunities to stay connected to their higher purpose. They joyfully embraced the challenges that come with organizational change because they knew that these obstacles enabled them to achieve their higher purpose. I am sure they had their moments of insecurity and frustration like me, but they never seemed to allow these human emotions to become obstacles on their journey. They placed leadership in its proper context—never larger than life. They viewed leadership and its obligations as merely one facet of their life experience. So many times leaders allow the storms to dictate their entire persona and, as a result, they lose sight of the inherent need of their employees to embrace a higher purpose above and beyond the context of their work lives. I think this reality has a lot to do with the growing level of employee dissatisfaction and burnout in corporate life today.

The desire for a higher purpose is innate in the human species. No one wants to fail. No one actively chooses a life of mediocrity. As simple and obvious as it may seem, this is an important frame of reference for leaders at any level. Acknowledging that not just some, but all of your employees strive for a higher purpose and value is an important building block of great leadership. Recognizing their values and promoting the synergy between organizational and employee values creates leadership success. So often we choose to see people in a single, one-dimensional context—defined largely by our own biases or their mundane and very limiting job titles. By contrast, great leadership allows us to see them as fellow travelers, citizens of the universe who share in the quest for higher purpose and value. Harnessing this higher purpose is one of the most important responsibilities of great leaders. It is also one of the greatest gifts of the leadership path. Well beyond increased shareholder value, leaders are presented with the opportunity to honor and nurture this gift in all employees, all fellow travelers. The irony in all of this is that absent the alignment of shared values and mutual respect, the sustained financial performance of most organizations is at best hit or miss. Winning is fleeting absent the gift of a higher purpose and its associated sense of community.

Beyond making good leadership look easy, highly successful leaders understand at a fundamental level that their success is not possible without the combined talent and efforts of many people. A dear friend and mentor once told me that much of my success as a leader came from being the conductor of a great orchestra. To me, her analogy means that, like a conductor, I was able to harness the collective talent, perspective, and uniqueness of a diverse group of people, which resulted in "making beautiful music" in the form of substantial financial success and customer retention. In hindsight, these outcomes were made possible by a conscious effort to honor and nurture the pursuit of a higher purpose both in myself and in my teammates.

My characterization of great leaders is central to the insights in this book. While my friend calls them great conductors, I refer to them as *Navigators*. Navigators make leadership look easy by handling the challenges that follow from organizational change with calm confidence. Because their inner guidepost or conscience is connected to a higher purpose, they can navigate the shifting currents of business without second-guessing themselves or micromanaging their people.

Through my period of reflection and discovery, I examined the many common traits of Navigators. I present my insights in a context that is intended to build on the strengths and perspectives that have brought you to the point of reading this book. There is no hard-and-fast rule for every leadership obstacle. Unique challenges require novel solutions. But, when you combine the lessons of this book with your life and leadership insights, you will be well on your way to becoming a Navigator both in and out of the space you call *work*. In being open to tapping the wisdom of your head, heart, and spirit, you will discover your own magic formula that will guide you on your path to great leadership. *Bon Voyage!*

—DAVID O'BRIEN
Bloomfield, CT
August 26, 2007

CHAPTER ONE

BEHAVIOR & CHOICE

"The opposite of leader is not follower,
it's pessimist" —Unknown

A fter my last corporate job as senior vice president and general manager of an international consulting firm in the field of workplace management services, a much-needed sabbatical was welcome. This time off for reflection was driven by a desire to assess what was learned about leadership and team dynamics over the previous twenty-five years in corporate America. The most important lesson discovered in this time of reflection was so simple it's hard to believe that it wasn't discovered until the sabbatical. While several factors influenced my career success or failure over the previous twenty-five years, it all came down to behavior. It may seem obvious, but how one behaves in the wake of controversial management decisions, organizational change, and shifting business expectations determines career success or failure. You have a choice: Navigate through the maze of complex emotions and behave in ways that maximize your standing in the company; or react negatively to the "corporate dragon" and thus undermine your standing in the company and potential for career satisfaction.

The choice to focus more on behaviors than attitudes or perceptions represents the foundation of this book. To be sure, perceptions and attitudes influence behavior, but ultimately our behaviors determine a great deal about our options. The first step is to recognize that regardless of our attitudes about controversial workplace changes or leadership decisions, our success or failure hinges on our behavior. Great leaders know when to behave in ways that don't necessarily jibe with their attitudes for the sake of moving the organizational goals forward. Also, leaders know that their best producers may not agree with everything their managers ask them to do, but choose to behave in ways that promote organizational goals anyway. *At the end of the day, leaders reward results.* Of course, it is always easy to behave in ways that promote organizational goals when your attitudes are in line with the company's values. The challenge often lies in choosing to behave contrary to your own attitudes for the sake of your team. Or better yet, recognizing that your own attitudes—and the behaviors that follow—are the cause of the problem, and choosing to bring your attitudes in line with organizational values and goals.

THE FOUR BEHAVIORS

Behaviors play out in both good and bad ways. Some astute folks have climbed the corporate ladder not from their genius or energy, but simply because they've reacted to difficult management decisions in ways that diffused conflict and produced results. More commonly over the years, many highly skilled people have unwittingly derailed their own careers and dreams by responding to initiatives in ways that amplified conflict and undercut desired results. I call these bad or negative behaviors *Detour Behaviors*. Over time and when compounded, detour behaviors serve as major impediments to career satisfaction, progress, and credibility.

As most people first discover this important success/failure link, they are not entirely clear about how to categorize these behaviors, or, for that matter, if they have some magical, universal application. Like many people, I am often suspicious of various theories on human behavior that attempt to define complex human beings as neatly fitting into three or four convenient boxes labeled by style or personality type.

Over the past seven years, I have tested the behavioral profiles described below with more than 2,000 leadership and line personnel from nearly every industry on three continents. The result of this informal validation process resulted in the unexpected. The original assessment that there were in fact four well-defined boxes for our behavioral choices was widely accepted as both accurate and meaningful. More than ninety percent of those surveyed strongly connected with these categories. The author also learned from this process that the detour behavior concept represented a more common and broader range of choices than the success-oriented behavioral choice. In nearly every example, the dominant behavior that most greatly influenced success is defined below as the *Navigator* behavior. By contrast, detour behaviors are defined as the *Victim, Critic,* and *Bystander* behaviors. The net of these behavioral choices encompasses more than just work-related difficulties, but on an even larger scale, life obstacles. After years of testing, it became obvious that these behavior types do have universal application.

THE VICTIM BEHAVIOR CHOICE

The first and possibly most destructive detour behavior that people embrace at one point or another in their careers (or lives) is the *Victim*. In this role, they believe that all of their obstacles, challenges, frustrations, and failures are directly related to some larger force that finds great pleasure in making their work life difficult. "They don't care about me, they don't value me, it's me against them" are all part of their internal belief system—a belief system that serves no value or benefit in their pursuit of career success. As flawed as it may seem, some victims actually imagine that a Department of Employee Complication exists at corporate headquarters. They are convinced that it is staffed by overpaid bean counters—men and woman in pinstripes who probably work from 10:00 a.m. to 2:00 p.m. three days per week. They imagine them sitting around plush offices contemplating how to make employee's lives difficult. These bean counters likely have the best of everything, including flowered terraces, gas grills for weekly barbecues, hourly coffee breaks, and, more than likely, bigger bonuses than the victim—all incentives designed to fuel their sinister plot.

Victims embrace a negative view of the world around them. They expend great amounts of energy in validating why their lives are a series of one failure or obstacle after another. Instead of owning up to their role in all of this, they opt to blame others for their unfortunate circumstances. Obviously, they are not able to rise above these attitudes to behave in ways that benefit their teams or themselves. Instead, they take pleasure in undermining the initiatives that they believe were designed to make their lives miserable. It never occurs to them that if they quit complaining about how overworked they are, and instead meet or exceed their manager's expectations for them, they might actually be given what they think they truly deserve: praise, recognition, and even a bonus or raise. So they continue to under-perform and blame their managers or coworkers for the lack of recognition or credibility.

Often, victims were once well-intentioned, partially engaged team members. They didn't just grow a third eye overnight. They evolved (or devolved) into victims from a higher species—a transition across the shifting tides of work and life change, pressure, ambiguity, and most of all poor leadership. It also is a transition across values and their associated belief system—rough seas to be sure. But most people have found themselves tossed on these seas from time to time not just in work, but outside of work too—including myself.

The continued exploration of the behavioral success/failure link, especially around the victim behavior, produced another unexpected benefit. Was it possible that difficulties outside of work could be influenced by a work-induced victim view of the world? Most victims are heavily invested in this behavior and all of its self-adsorbing limitations. After spending ten or twelve hours at work each day stuck in the victim mode, it is next to impossible to fully switch gears upon arrival home.

THE CRITIC BEHAVIOR CHOICE

A close relative to the victim is the *Critic*. Critics often suffer from an ego that does not match their accomplishments. They typically think that they could do much better than their managers. Because critics are so sure that their managers are incompetent, they jump to the conclusion that whatever new initiative comes along must be another in a string of managerial blunders. Rather than giving their supervisors the benefit of the doubt or trying to see their points of view, they automatically criticize initiatives and work to undermine their success.

Critics are sure that all their difficulties and challenges are some specific person's fault: the boss, a coworker whom the boss favors, the CEO, the marketing VP, the CFO, a new customer. A common lament for the critic is "Things just aren't like they used to be around here." They crave the familiar and cling to the past hoping that if they just hold on long enough things will get better and the good old days will return. Little do they know that change is a necessary part of growth and that the change dragon only gets bigger and faster as market forces and shareholder demands increase.

Like victims, critics often embrace a negative view of the world around them. They too spend a lot of energy validating their drudgery. They avoid reality by convincing themselves and others around them that all of their problems or difficulties are some one else's fault. To get others to buy into their negative impressions of management, they often become master manipulators—folks who work the system to their benefit and at times, to the benefit of their fellow critics. When in high gear, critics work overtime at fostering a culture of cynics. They are convinced that their read on things is both accurate and more enlightened than management's.

Part of the critic validation process involves not only preaching these flawed insights about how everyone else is wrong or against us. It also involves looking for ways to sabotage progress. Most critics gain great satisfaction from being able to say "I told you so." They invest a lot of time and energy in building consensus around their beliefs. They wear the critic label as a badge of honor. Finding flaws in new initiatives, systems, or processes serves as another form of validation that ultimately fuels their convictions about just how wrong the organization is, and just how right they are in their internal belief system.

A senior-level coaching client I was working with a few years ago had enjoyed a meteoric rise to divisional president as part of a merger. By all accounts he was the best choice for the role. Shortly after taking the helm of this venture, he began to have daily conflicts with the new parent company's executive team over how things used to be done prior to the merger. Instead of looking for ways to learn and adapt—let alone increase the new company's investment—he opted to criticize every aspect of the new culture, including its systems and operational policies. This critic behavior nearly cost him his job. Early in our coaching process I asked him what percentage of the problems were the parent company's fault and what percentage was his fault. He replied that it was ninety percent them and only ten percent him. As you might imagine, the reverse was much more likely the case. What appeared to be intentional, corporate-sponsored roadblocks to his success were in fact more sophisticated methods of achieving increased shareholder value and return on the parent company's investment. Not only did he believe that there was a department of employee complication at corporate headquarters, he was convinced that the new executive team was out to get him. To complicate things, this flawed view of the new partnership began to surface among the divisional president's direct reports, and in a matter of only months a culture of *us ver-sus them* was alive and well in the division. Once I helped him understand his role in this counter-productive culture, he turned it around and saved his job in the process.

THE MISERY-LOVES-COMPANY BUS

Once you've spent considerable time as a victim or critic the *misery-loves-company* bus shows up on the workplace scene. After all, it's not as much fun to go the victim or critic route alone. Why not build a community of psychic vampires who thrive on stealing the good energy of those coworkers who seem to be engaged, having fun, or making progress? Often, the *misery—loves-company* bus is driven by the chief victim or critic of the work group or team. They take great pride in their new found status as the official or unofficial spokesperson for the team. Some bus drivers are so into the power and recognition associated with being the ring leader that they offer inducements for getting on the bus. Coffee time, lunch meetings and even heightened social status are but a few of the attractions of joining the *misery-loves-company* bus crowd. Often this is all it takes to convert those employees who are subjected to poor leadership day after day and who at some level feel disenfranchised with the organizational direction. The sense of community connected to this crowd becomes a powerful force that over time erodes even a good leader's ability to produce meaningful results. When it occurs under the watch of a dysfunctional leader, the obstacles to success are magnified on a grand scale.

THE BYSTANDER BEHAVIOR CHOICE

When the bus route conflicts with some part of our belief system for a long enough time, we engage in the next detour behavior—the *Bystander.* Often, the transition from victim to critic to bystander is a relatively slow process. It doesn't happen overnight. Over time the first two behaviors zap much of your energy, drive, and commitment and essentially you unplug from your workplace experience. Oh sure, you show up every day and are physically there, but your heart and head are somewhere else.

The bystander is the classic side-lines player who is anything but engaged or committed. It happens in those team members who give and give but rarely get feedback, let alone praise. It happens in those team members who go the extra mile for you but then look around and notice that they're the only ones working late or working through lunch. It happens when team members are not challenged enough and get bored with their jobs. In most cases, bystanders evolve from victims or critics when they lose credibility with their managers and their managers fail to engage them.

Bystanders, in many ways, represent a greater challenge for leaders than the first two detour behaviors. Unlike victims and critics, bystanders rarely wear the badge of honor associated with this behavior. In most cases, victims and critics form small (and sometimes large) subcultures within organizations complete with some level of hierarchy, status, and even reward systems. After all, misery does love company. By contrast, bystanders don't make waves and play the game fairly well. They're not even engaged enough to be critical. They show up and count the minutes and hours until quitting time, or even worse, the minutes and hours until retirement.

While bystanders don't necessarily spend large amounts of energy validating their workplace beliefs, they often do have a deeply rooted view that is similar to victims and critics. Like the first two detour behaviors, bystanders are suspicious of management and the overall direction of the organization. They have seen managers come and go and have also had their share of new initiatives, systems, or processes, all of which have failed to make their work experience better by their measure. "It's just another management fad," "It's not my job," and "I'm too busy" are all part of the bystanders' operating language. Like victims, bystanders also have the potential to be manipulators. You have likely seen many people over the years who appear to be well engaged and successful team players. On the surface, they appear to be very busy, driven, and even dedicated to the common good of the team or organization. Just below the surface, however, lies a skillful manipulator who invests great energy in beating the system or creating complex schemes for coasting through their work day. When it comes time to produce meaningful and consistent results, they come up short on your expectations and often have a multitude of excuses for why they didn't get things done. Bystanders are also masterful at passing the buck. They resist accountability, and, like victims at some level, prefer to blame others for their circumstances. Because they are often former victims or critics, they often revert to those behaviors under pressure.

Most bystanders share another characteristic or trait of victims. They operate from a *me* or *us versus them* belief system. I think a large part of this comes from feeling isolated from the mainstream. Maybe this has its roots in earlier life or work experiences. Nonetheless, this belief system fosters poor productivity and career distress. The career distress component is a common link to each of the three detour behaviors. Most of this distress comes from the impact that the detour behaviors have on a person's reputation and ultimate success.

Once employees acquire the victim, critic, or bystander label, it's difficult to reverse that legacy in the minds of their leaders.

Several years ago I was conducting a series of change-management training classes for a major financial services client that had seen its share of transformation and chaos—driven largely by external market conditions. During the needs-assessment phase of the training project, I learned that many employees felt that they were stuck in dead-end jobs with little or no hope for vertical movement within the organization. When I pressed for more clarity around this perception, the head of Human Resources indicated that there were in fact many vehicles for development and advancement within the organization but that most of these resources were underutilized or, at best, seen by employees as "token initiatives to keep the team happy." Upon further review, I learned that frontline managers did not invest the time or energy in helping to develop their people. This led to a lack of participation in career development resources. After conducting several training sessions for these frontline managers, a bigger issue emerged. Frontline managers failed to encourage their people to use the resources because they thought of their people as victims, critics, or bystanders. Once again, employees behaved badly; this led to bad reputations and, ultimately, career distress.

In my first line-personnel training session, I solicited input from participants regarding how the detour behaviors played out for them at work. What had been a rather nebulous discussion quickly blossomed into a sense of clarity that allowed participants to see first-hand how their behaviors affected their reputations. It also helped them see how their behavior was driving their feelings of career distress. I created a little game with them that further illustrated the behavior/reputation link. We identified an imaginary new initiative in which each of them would be required to devote an additional 10 hours per week without delegating any of their other work duties. Participants were asked to define how each of the three behavioral types would respond to the new initiative and increased work demands. Within minutes they were able to witness how the behaviors played out and quickly discovered the link between their detour behaviors and career distress.

THE NAVIGATOR BEHAVIOR CHOICE

By now you have likely identified the behavioral profiles of many members of your team, and maybe even your peer group or external social system. Look around, the people who are making it happen every day, the ones who manage to produce day in and day out, the ones who expertly surf the waves of change—even against tough odds—these are your *Navigators*. Navigators respond to challenging behaviors from others in the work environment with calm confidence, diffusing negative energy and infusing their teams with exuberance and gumption. They seize the opportunity in daily obstacles and, above all, produce lasting value to their teams and their organizations.

THE NAVIGATOR'S NORTH STAR

As mentioned earlier, my sabbatical from corporate life provided a wonderful opportunity to assess the lessons and truths about leadership and success. While the three detour behaviors are paramount to failure as a leader or individual contributor, the single most powerful thread that surfaced again and again in the major success stories from coaching clients was choosing to be a *Navigator*—the fourth behavior. As much as I would like to be able to say that I knowingly chose this behavioral option at every juncture of my career, I cannot. In fact, most of the time it was just simply "taking the high road." This high-road concept is most clearly connected to our internal guidepost, *our conscience, the Navigator's North Star.* It tells us time after time that what was right ten or twenty or even thirty years ago still is right today. It's also about honoring all that we have invested in our careers, including sacrifice, hard work, and perseverance. We'll discuss the high-road concept, including the connection between our internal guidepost and effective leadership, in more detail in a later chapter. For now, suffice it to say that these are important building blocks of the Navigator.

Just as engaging in detour behaviors doesn't happen overnight but is the culmination of a lengthy string of bad experiences, becoming a navigator doesn't happen overnight either. Leaders and producers start taking the high road, realize how it improves outcomes, and gradually develop other traits of navigators. It isn't simply avoiding detour behaviors but choosing to behave in ways that align the higher purpose of the organization with the values of the individual. Becoming a full-time Navigator is a journey that itself requires navigation. Creating a culture of Navigators begins with you!

The journey of the Navigator represents a continuum of behaviors from Junior Navigators to Master Navigators, and everything in between. Junior Navigators are full of hope and promise but still in need of consistent good leadership. Junior Navigators are a manager's dream. They're willing to help others on the team without seeking a reward. They're willing to accept difficult assignments because they know that the job needs to be done. And while they're not afraid to ask questions about where the department or company is headed (and they may not agree with the answers they're given) they don't let these feelings get in the way of their performance. Master Navigators are those that everyone looks to for guidance. They never miss an opportunity to inspire their people to bring their values in line with the higher organizational purpose, creating generations of Junior Navigators in the process. Master Navigators are easy to pick out. Everyone respects them. Everyone looks up to them. Everyone wants to follow them. Not that they're always right—everyone makes mistakes. But they are the first to admit their mistakes and lay out ways to avoid them in the future. This breeds the respect of their people and the whole organization.

Unlike the other behavior types, Navigators take ownership and pride in their work. They have a strong desire to contribute to and participate in the success of their organization. While at many levels they don't allow ambiguity or dissent to cloud their judgment and corresponding behavioral response, they don't simply say "yes" to every initiative that comes along. Often, Navigators seek to challenge the status quo not for the sake of being difficult, but ultimately for the higher good of their team and their organization. The clarity and commitment stems from their core values and their own inner guidepost. Navigators can become vulnerable to the detour behaviors when leaders persistently make decisions that are in conflict with the Navigators' belief systems or inner guideposts. Let's face it, not all managers got where they are by being Navigators. Many get there merely through length of service, others through manipulation.

Junior Navigators who persevere under difficult managers must pick their battles. But they risk veering off into detour behaviors if they never dissent to unethical or unfeasible initiatives.

Just as Junior Navigators must challenge their leaders from time to time, full-fledged Navigators must listen to their people when they object to the direction the team is going. Sometimes this can be difficult because some folks have radically different perspectives grounded in different cultures, religions, and families of origin. A common denominator in my success as a leader came from not just treating people as I wanted to be treated, but ultimately honoring and nurturing their differences. Countless organizations preach this openness and commitment to their "greatest asset," but few take the time to put these words into action. Honoring and nurturing differences is not a complicated science but actually much more of an art. It seems like a contradiction to say that you want your employees to share your core values and yet have diverse backgrounds. But the two are compatible. People can have diverse backgrounds yet share the same core values. What distinguishes them are not the values themselves but the way they express their values. Diverse teams are less prone to mistakes because the different perspectives on their core values are self-correcting.

In addition to these characteristics, Navigators are change hardy and resilient in the wake of today's shifting workplace currents. They embrace change and ultimately see it as an opportunity for improved performance and personal development. They communicate important developments in a timely fashion and look to assist those team members who struggle with the new workplace realities. After all, the four behaviors are intimately linked to change management. While it is important to navigate during calm seas, it becomes increasingly important when the winds of change are at gale force. The rougher the seas, the more your team needs you to navigate. Still, there are many insights about change management that need to be addressed in a separate chapter later in this book.

Great leadership is all about bringing out the best in ourselves and our teammates. Clearly, this doesn't just happen but rather takes time, energy, lots of communication and commitment. It has been my observation both as a consultant and a senior leader that nearly all employees show up at work each day with some desire to be successful. They have an inner success factor that is either ignored or silenced by poor leadership. Despite my strong investment in my various detour behaviors over my career, I never once had a daily work or life-related goal to fail. I honestly don't think anyone does. In this reality lies one of the most powerful and meaningful opportunities for leaders to build a navigator culture. If we accept and even embrace this thinking, we can take the first step towards bringing out the best in our people and ourselves.

THE FOUR BEHAVIORS *At A Glance*

✳ VICTIM:

What They Feel—Shock, Grief, Loss,
Anger, Disbelief, Frustration
What They Do—Avoid, Withdraw, Resist,
Sabotage, Challenge Progress & Decisions
What They Say—I can't believe this is happening,
Poor me, They don't understand or value me

✳ CRITIC:

What They Feel—Anger, Resentment,
Insecure, Confused, Entitled
What They Do—Blame, Act-out, Overreact, Disrupt
What They Say—This place isn't what it
used to be, They don't know what
they're doing, No one cares

✳ BYSTANDER:

What They Feel—Shock, Frustration, Disengaged,
Removed, Out of touch with reality
What They Do—Show-up, Avoid, Resist,
Manipulate, Ignore, Unplug
What They Say—It's not my job, I'm too busy, This
is just another management fad, I'm tired

✳ NAVIGATOR:

What They Feel—Energized, Collaborative,
Focused, Optimistic, Hopeful
What They Do—Own their jobs, Help
others, Seize the opportunity, Move
forward, Support progress
What They Say—Let's try this, We can do it,
We've been successful before, It's up to us

Exercises FOR BUILDING A NAVIGATOR CULTURE

1. Utilizing the four behavior model, assess the profile of your core team for purposes of defining the behavioral mix and associated challenges and opportunities. Using the same assessment process, define the behavioral profile of your leadership peer group.

2. Encourage all leadership personnel to explore how the four behaviors play out among the leadership team including the impact that each behavior has on morale and employee engagement.

3. Solicit feedback from all team members on how the four behaviors affect their personal satisfaction and individual success.

4. Encourage open communication around the four behaviors including candid feedback on how the detour behaviors play out among the team. Ask team members to explore their successes and failures over the past year or so to explore how the four behaviors have influenced theses outcomes.

LESSONS FROM THE NAVIGATOR'S NOTEBOOK

1. At the end of the day, leaders reward results.

2. Behaviors play out in both good and bad ways.

3. Over time, detour behaviors serve as major impediments to career success.

4. Victims believe that someone else is responsible for their failures.

5. When in high gear, Critics work to create a culture of cynics.

6. The Bystander is the classic side-lines player who is anything but engaged.

7. The "misery-loves-company" bus is alive and well in most companies today.

8. The journey of the Navigator is a continuum of behaviors.

9. The Navigator's North Star is most often the soul or conscience.

10. Master Navigators inspire people to align their values with a higher purpose.

WHAT'S YOUR INTERNAL SCREEN?

"True leaders are dispensers of hope" —*Napoleon*

In early 2002 I was doing a two-day team-building retreat for a client in Washington D.C. when I had what I would describe as another major discovery related to the four behaviors discussed in the last chapter. After completing the first day of the program, I joined the program participants for dinner and what proved to be some very stimulating conversation around the topic of leadership and the four behaviors. I left the dinner feeling deeply connected to the team, not just on a leadership or career level but, perhaps more importantly, on a human level. We were all very much invested in what we were doing at this point in our lives, but we also shared another powerful bond—we each sought clarity around *how* and *why* the four behaviors manifest themselves in and out of work.

Upon arriving back at my hotel that evening, I began to ponder the clarity issue regarding the four behaviors. As I fell asleep, I had this strong sense that my dreams would follow this pursuit of clarity. At approximately 3:00 a.m., I awoke with one very clear and almost startling picture in my mind. It was a sign that read, WMIS AM & FM.

I didn't have a clue as to where this was coming from, let alone what it was supposed mean. I'm not a fan of radio stations much anyway, and I rarely find the time to watch CNN or the local news when I'm traveling on business, so exploring the local radio selection is not an option. Besides, I had not even managed to catch the local radio on my taxi ride from the airport to my hotel the day before. As I struggled to find meaning in this sleep induced discovery, I found myself getting frustrated by the fact that I sensed some strong and meaningful relevance to my dinner conversation but yet had no idea, no clue, as to its meaning. After nearly two hours of tossing and turning, I finally fell back to sleep for what was likely not more than forty-five minutes before my wake-up call summoned me to day two of my team-building program. Within seconds of adjusting my eyes to the daylight rushing through the partially closed curtains of my hotel room, a stream of consciousness struck me like a freight train. The answer to my 3:00 a.m. puzzle became clear. The link to our dinner conversation was real *and* very meaningful.

WHAT'S MY INTERNAL SCREEN?

For years I had believed that every day we awake to an internal screen in our mind that greatly influences how we start our day, and even more importantly where we let it go. I had been certain that if we challenged our early morning assumptions a bit, we could in fact alter at some level or another the type of day we had. So often we awake to the normal human feelings of being tired, achy, and stressed by the enormous amount of things we need to do in our short day. Work issues, family issues, car and house issues, dreams and opportunities missed. These all have the potential to fuel our frustration around another day, another challenge, *and another day in the rat race.* It influences how we connect or don't connect with key people in our lives—beginning with the very first interaction of the day, and more than likely right up to and including the last interaction of the day.

After pondering this reality for much of the night, the WMIS AM & FM mystery began to unravel. With almost the same level of intensity as my 3:00 a.m. experience, I now saw that the first part of the mystery was in fact a question, a probe, or even a reality check. *What's My Internal Screen?* Alas, the WMIS, the screen that we tune into at that first moment of consciousness every day. The place where our energy either gets sapped or zapped, the place where joy and hope are either embraced or extinguished. Is it about failure, regret and apprehension—the *Frustration Mode,* or FM, of my experience, or is it about gratitude and joy for another opportunity to experience a new day, a new beginning. This, I discovered, was the *Appreciation Mode* or AM of the puzzle.

The foundation of the Appreciation Mode goes beyond gratitude and joy. I honestly think it begins with an inner awareness around just how many blessings and or gifts we have in our lives at any given moment. I remember a situation with a colleague of mine many years ago who had just been laid off from his job with a major financial services employer in New Jersey after only five months. He had been out of work from a previous job lay off for nearly a year when he landed what appeared to be this fabulous executive job that was only ten miles from his home. After only three months on the job, he was asked to relocate in order to take on an even larger role within the company. Despite his family's objections about moving, he sold his house and was living in temporary housing while his children finished the school year. After only six weeks in the new job, he was called into his boss's office one day and without warning informed that his position was being eliminated due to a company-wide cost savings initiative. All of his hopes and dreams were dashed in a matter of seconds. In his words, he felt as if "the whole world had come crashing down around him." Beyond the thought of losing another job in such a short period of time and the fact that he was no longer in his forties was the fact that he had sold the family house only one month before this dreadful day. How could he possibly tell his wife and children that his decision to uproot them was such a disaster?

As is so often the case in corporate life today, this decent human being was escorted out of the building and told that his personal belongings would be forwarded to him in a few days. To add insult to injury, his boss told him that he would have to vacate the company apartment by the end of the week. Overwhelmed with fear, anger, and resentment, he proceeded to make the three-hour commute back to his family in Connecticut. As he drove north on the New Jersey Turnpike, the reality of what had just occurred began to sink in. He began to feel desperate and actually contemplated taking his life. In this darkest of dark moments, he somehow drew strength from his inner guidepost that told him that he would some how, some way get through this. Not entirely convinced by this inner guidepost, he decided to make a list of all the things that he had to be thankful for, all the things that were blessings in his life at that very moment. His first entry on a fast-food napkin that he pulled from his glove box was, "My wiper blades are working."

As he reached the George Washington Bridge, he came upon a heavy downpour and at that first moment of gratitude he realized that working wiper blades were for sure a good thing, a blessing. Over the next thirty minutes, he had compiled a list of over forty things that he had to be thankful for at that very moment. Sure there were some rather mundane items like the wiper blades and a full tank of gas, but there were also some powerful items like family, health, faith, friends, and love. What started as a major challenge to his inner guidepost quickly blossomed into a frame of mind that was heavily anchored in gratitude and hope, the essence of the Appreciation Mode. Over the next several months and with a lot of help from friends and family, he launched his own consulting firm, which to this day continues to be not just a thriving business, but ultimately a blessing that put him on the right path.

Our choice to examine our blessings is often more about making a daily, focused effort and less about waiting for a disaster like my colleague experienced. Like so many people including myself, we get stuck on the FM screen in those first few moments of consciousness each day and rarely take the time to change the channel.

Being stuck in the FM mode goes deeper than the simple frustrations associated with another day in the rat race. I think this deeper element has its roots in fear, which by my estimate is the active partner of the Frustration Mode. We fear that things won't go our way, that people won't like us, that we'll never really be happy or win at the game of life. Fear makes us shrink on the playing field of life, and as leaders greatly inhibits our ability to lead, influence, and inspire our people. How can we as leaders possibly honor and nurture our people when we're in the FM mode?

So often we allow the FM to dictate our day and how we choose to operate within its boundaries. When I thought further back to my victim and critic experiences, I saw this as a powerful connection that fueled my detour behavior. How could I possibly take the "high road," or for that matter even tap into my internal guidepost of knowledge and wisdom, when I was shrinking on the path of fear and frustration. How many well intentioned leaders of people miss this key ingredient all together? I know from my research as well as my own experience that the answer to this is *too many.* We hire people with promise, we invest in them, we promote them and then we extinguish their hope by tuning out the AM channel and tuning into the FM channel on our daily screen. Sure, it's more than this, but I am convinced that it remains a very real and major impediment to great leadership and all of its many rewards.

When we choose the FM screen we unknowingly choose a narrow view rife with more obstacles than we attempted to avoid in the first place. The FM channel I believe creates a barrier around us that prevents us from being grounded, feeling love and experiencing joy. It also prevents us from sharing these gifts and in the long run can extinguish our hope if we allow it to. As leaders in any part of life, we can never be too grounded or hopeful. We can also never bring too much joy to our work or personal lives. Being grounded and choosing to change the channel to AM also allows us to be our best in all of our roles. I can't begin to count the times over my career or for that matter the past few years when the FM channel prevented me from doing my absolute best, from being the leader, parent or friend that I want to be and am capable of being. Sadly, the FM channel knows no boundaries. It can have a hugely negative impact on all areas of our life. By contrast, on those days when we awake to the AM channel, we somehow see a broader range of options for dealing with our daily human challenges. Out of the Appreciation Mode comes a sense of quiet confidence or optimism that assures us that some how, some way, we can not only get through this, but it also might just be enjoyable. It also invites more good into our day and helps us to stay grounded.

One important consideration for feeding the AM screen is acknowledging that *we are and always will be bigger than the sum of our daily or weekly challenges.* I remember a period of time when my darling wife had been more than a little overwhelmed by the demands of her mid-level leadership job. This is not to say that she's only felt overwhelmed once in her long distinguished Human Resources career, but rather this was an extended period of time when the pressures of a work-life balance seemed insurmountable. Every day started with a list of all the obstacles and distractions she faced on her way to creating impact and value at work. Sure I would manage to encourage her and offer various bits of Navigator wisdom along the way, but rarely was it more than a subtle attempt to be a good and caring partner.

Finally, one day I decided to challenge her internal screen. I asked in the middle of her litany of obstacles just how much her thinking, her screen, was influencing the obstacles, and ultimately, were all of these issues bigger than her? At first take, my wife responded that she could not change the fact that her boss kept raising the productivity bar at work and that the rate of organizational change had gone from rapid to "warp factor seven" in only a matter of months. The universal challenge of doing more with less was clearly taking its toll on her internal screen. It was also clouding her reality, which to a large extent had her convinced that the FM mode was her best survival mechanism.

As we began what turned out to be a series of discussions around the AM and FM choice, I asked her to think about the blessings or gifts in her life at that very moment. She was quick to respond that she had many blessings in her life including family, career, good friends, a beautiful home, and perhaps most importantly, good health. Sure these might seem obvious, but really, how often do we ignore these gifts and opt for the FM screen? This simple reality is not about living a fantasy life where we fail to acknowledge life's many challenges, but rather, it's about actively choosing to never let them have power over us. When our daily insecurities and obstacles become more powerful than our capacity to navigate and thus live in the AM mode, we need to take a serious look at what we're doing to create this outcome. So often our negative self talk and its associated self-defeating beliefs create boundaries that limit not just our capacity to navigate at work, but more importantly, at home.

As leaders and fellow travelers, we must challenge the flawed thinking that is our negative self talk. This leadership link represented a meaningful transition point for my wife over our series of discussions around the AM and FM choice. Over several weeks of almost daily discussions, my wife and I discovered that while her FM mode was by her estimates a reasonable survival mechanism for dealing with the corporate dragon, it also had profound impact on her ability to maintain a high level of team engagement at work.

Out of this important observation or reality check, we began to explore the link between her internal screen and how her team responded.

I'm sure this has been said a dozen different ways over the past 1000 years, but in our world, in our small way, we sum up this link as *the universe reciprocates.* I have had the benefit of reading many "human development" books over the years by such giants as Norman Vincent Peale, Og Mandino, and Claude Bristol, and despite no absolute connection to this metaphor, a common thread of wisdom in each literary gem is our power to influence our lives and the lives of others in a meaningful way. Another unwritten lesson that I've gleaned from these writers is the concept of good energy and bad energy that we put out in the world. The correlation to the universe reciprocates metaphor for my wife and I is simply this: when you put out good energy into the world, you often get good energy back. As you might imagine, this follows for bad energy, too. While I can't say that my wife chooses the AM channel every second of every day, I can say with gratitude that she has developed a new set of skills and perspective for managing the FM screen.

THE GIFT OF THE BLUE MARBLE

I had been working on three major projects simultaneously for over a month and was feeling more than a bit stretched and stressed. On top of this I had my usual work load of ongoing coaching and speaking assignments. I had all of the usual "life" things on my plate, too. I was at full throttle to say the least. One evening as I was saying good night to my six-year-old daughter, she informed me that she knew that I was tired and was more than a little concerned about all of the "weenies" (her word for negative people) out there in my work life. She went on to say that she had a special gift for me. Feeling a bit tired and rushed, I said something routine like, "Great, you can show it to me in the morning." After all, it was past her bed time and I still had a few hours of work to do to get ready for the next day. She insisted that I needed the gift right then and there and that I also needed to close my eyes and hold out my hand. Feeling frustrated, I complied with her wishes. When I opened my hand I discovered a blue marble. Still distracted by my pending workload, I said thank you and good night. As you might imagine, it didn't end there. She was excited to tell me that the blue marble was "the sum of all of my good energy" and that whenever I encountered a "weenie" all I needed to do was hold the marble tightly. It would neutralize the other person's bad energy, she informed me. What a gift indeed!

Five or so months before I received the blue marble, my daughter had overheard a conversation that I had with my wife about the universe reciprocates and the power of good and bad energy. She reminded me that shortly after that conversation she had asked me about it and that I had told her that it applied to her as well and that she had the same opportunity every day to choose to put out good energy instead of bad. She also quoted me as saying that I thought the world needed a lot more good energy. I think she's right.

Since the precious gift of the blue marble, I have not only carried the marble with me almost every day, but have also given the gift of a blue marble to many friends and associates. Beyond being a powerful reminder of the importance of good energy, it has served and continues to serve as a powerful link to the AM channel.

HEAVY TRAFFIC IS NOT A BAD THING

In the early 1990s I lived in a small town just south of the capital city where I was raised. I had just started my ten-year journey with my last employer and found myself on the road quite a bit. As I think back to that point in my career, I honestly believe that it was the first time that I fully accepted the Navigator path. While I certainly didn't label it this, I am certain that it was about taking the high road and tapping my internal guidepost frequently. I also now think that it had a lot to do with my internal screen. As a beginning point, I was very pleased to be part of the organization as it was at the time considered the standard bearer of quality and excellence in its industry. I also felt that my values and career goals were very much aligned with the culture and overall direction of the organization. Bigger than all of this was my occasional belief that my attitude influenced my career and life success. In retrospect, this may very well have been the infancy of the whole Navigator concept that has been so deeply ingrained in every aspect of my life these past seven years.

My work-related travels often found me driving past many nondescript buildings that lined the road near the entrance ramp to the major interstate highway in my area. So often I was oblivious to the various signs indicating the business's name or product, let alone vehicles entering or leaving their premises. One morning I just happened to be stuck in traffic near the small industrial park adjacent to the interstate and I noticed something that greatly influenced my internal screen. Exiting the driveway that I had passed one hundred times or more was a large flatbed truck that was carrying six burial vaults. As I looked at the truck, I noticed the company's sign, which clearly indicated that it was a burial vault manufacturing facility. Upon noticing this, my first thought was how lucky I was not to be their customer that day. None of those six large cement and steel vaults had my name on it. What little cues do you miss on any given day? I'm sure that like me there are many reminders, some as powerful as the burial vaults and some more subtle, like being able to get out of bed in the morning or wiper blades that work when it's raining.

I have discussed my **WMIS AM & FM** discovery with many people over the past few years, and while most people grasp it quickly, there are still those victims and critics out there (like I've been more than once) who prefer to believe that the FM channel is not only very practical but actually an important self-survival mechanism. After all, they need some way of dealing with the weird people who seem to be having fun at one level or another in and out of work. Please know that the AM channel is not something that I tune into the first second of every day. Rather, most mornings find me dealing with the same set of issues I mentioned before, including family and career-related items that often take front and center stage. Other mornings it's the ego-driven insecurities of getting older, less attractive, thinner on top, and not quite as agile as I once was. Most days I find it entirely too easy to stay in the FM zone. It takes work to shift, after ten seconds or ten minutes of self-induced fear in the FM zone. The negatives have this mysterious way of feeding the FM screen to the point where some mornings I'm nearly convinced that the AM screen is fantasy land. It's not! It is a place where any one of us can choose to hang out, to explore at any given moment, not just any given day.

Group Activities FOR BUILDING A NAVIGATOR CULTURE

1. Explore what the AM & FM channels mean in your life. What influence do they have on your team's perspective and level of engagement?

2. How many blessings do you have in your life at this very moment? How many people including your team members know the extent of these blessings?

3. Incorporate a discussion around the AM & FM channels with your team and ask them to define how each impacts collaboration and team satisfaction.

4. Solicit feedback from team members on how the AM & FM screens influence the four behaviors and ultimately the team's long-term success.

5. Keep a journal for 30 days that captures your thoughts and feelings relative to the AM & FM channels. What can you do to increase the AM time by 10% next month?

Chapter Two

LESSONS FROM THE
NAVIGATOR'S NOTEBOOK

1. Every day we awake to an internal screen in our head that greatly influences how we start our day and where we let it go.

2. Challenging our early morning assumptions can alter the direction of our day.

3. Our internal screen influences how we connect or don't connect with the key people in our life.

4. The FM screen is heavily anchored in fear, regret and failure.

5. The AM screen is heavily anchored in gratitude, hope and joy.

6. So often we allow the FM screen to define our day and who we are.

7. We can't tap our inner guidepost when we shrink on the path of fear and frustration.

8. We are and always will be bigger than the sum of our daily or weekly challenges.

9. Our negative self talk creates huge barriers that limit our ability to Navigate.

10. The Universe Reciprocates

The EVOLUTION of
LEADERSHIP

"The first responsibility of a leader is to define reality; the last is to say thank you" —Max DePree

Following my keynote speech, Robert approached me and asked if I thought Paula's new boss had a hidden agenda. I had just delivered a keynote presentation on the evolution of leadership to an annual convention of state leaders and had told Paula's story to illustrate a point about employee satisfaction. Paula had been with a local employer for twenty-six years, and had by all accounts done her job very well. She was the one that people looked to not just for her technical expertise, but also for her keen insight into the political landscape of her work environment. Unfortunately, Paula had been working for a boss who constantly belittled her and her colleagues, and who by most measures was a very negative and controlling manager. After a dozen years of working for this woman, Paula had become a bit of a victim and critic, which over time led to some very obvious bystander behaviors. She had hoped to retire after thirty years but her "toxic" manager made that reality seem like the impossible dream.

One day and without any warning, Paula's boss

resigned. I remember her telling me that it was one of the best things that ever happened to her and her co-workers. Within a month of this person's departure, Paula had a new boss who seemed like the complete opposite of the last boss. One day shortly after he joined the team, he invited Paula to lunch at a very nice restaurant. In all of her twenty-six previous years, no boss had ever taken her to lunch. Over lunch, her new boss explained that he recognized her talent, perspective, and history and saw her playing a key role in the success of the team. He also took the time to learn about her interests and family life. My point to Robert and his colleagues was that I thought that Paula's new manager had made a very smart investment in taking her to lunch and more importantly expressing his view that he saw her playing a key role in the success of the department.

Robert's perspective, influenced greatly by his view of leadership, was that the new manager must have had a "hidden agenda" when he took Paula to lunch. I was a bit perplexed so I inquired as to what he thought the "hidden agenda" might be. "He was just trying to push her buttons. He wanted to get her to work harder. Now she'll expect positive feedback all the time," he lamented. Clearly, expecting positive feedback when it's warranted is not a bad thing. Wanting an employee to work harder isn't a bad thing either. Pushing people's buttons just for the sake of pushing their buttons is.

Robert had lived through more than his fair share of bad managers. He had worked at his employer for nearly forty years and "had been in a leadership role for as long as he could remember." His view of leadership was very much anchored in the old command and control model of management. He seemed to believe that employees needed to be controlled and managed. Needless to say, the concept of Navigating and taking the high road was at best a very foreign concept that in his mind did not belong in the workplace of 1967 or 2007 for that matter.

American social psychologist and researcher Douglas McGregor in his 1960 book entitled *The Human Side of Enterprise* defined two models of leadership that have a strong link to Robert's view of leadership and my thinking relative to the Navigator's path. He described the Theory X leadership model as being born out of the industrial revolution where people needed to be controlled and managed. Some of the assumptions that fueled the Theory X view of leadership included:

* People have a natural dislike for work and will avoid it when possible
* People must be controlled and coerced
* People have little or no ambition
* Threats and punishment are key motivators
* Workers can't be trusted

By contrast, McGregor defined leadership Theory Y as a model that encompassed a new and more realistic view that shifted the thinking from managing people to leading people. The foundational thinking that embodied the Theory Y view of leadership included:

* People want to succeed
* People will exercise self-direction if given the opportunity
* People seek responsibility
* Creativity, ingenuity and motivation are inherent in all people
* Workers want to be trusted

The leadership behavior link to both models is very powerful. It starts with your internal screen and perspective about your employees and then transcends all interactions with every member of your team. Clearly, Leadership Theory Y is all about the Navigator path.

While McGregor's Theory Y dates back to a very different time in corporate America, much of its assumptions serve as important reminders for successful leaders today. A parallel view that not only encompasses his Theory Y model but also my Navigator model includes the following foundational guideposts:

* Nobody wants to fail
* People want to be valued and make a difference
* Clarity and purpose are basic human motivators
* Leadership is an opportunity that must be honored
* Leadership excellence is a journey and not a destination

In acknowledging that not a single person on your team wants to fail, you begin to trust a bit more. Trust is a critical element of Theory Y and the Navigator's thinking. In the earlier case of my discussion with Robert, he clearly felt that he could not trust Paula's boss with his "hidden agenda" nor could he trust Paula to stay focused and not be overly needy around the issue of praise and recognition. "She'll expect positive feedback all the time," he surmised.

Trust is a huge responsibility, leadership is too. We'll explore this in more detail later, but for now I want to share some observations from a wide range of learning related to how leadership has evolved. Like in the keynote address I mentioned earlier, I often include a group exercise that I call "Exploring Your Perspective" in my leadership training classes. In this exercise, I ask folks to identify not just how they have seen leadership evolve over their careers, but also what characteristics best describe the good and bad leaders that they have worked for over time.

While there are always some strong parallels on both parts of the exercise, the most striking learning for me is that the top five or so *good leadership* characteristics are almost predicable. *Respect, Trust, Integrity, Fairness,* and *Professionalism* almost always show up as the top five and in every case show up in the top ten of the positive leadership characteristics. There are some equally strong similarities with the bad leadership characteristics with *Controlling, Disrespect, Condescending, Unethical* and *Micro manages* as the consistently highly ranked characteristics of bad leaders. Following on the next page is a snapshot of what hundreds of seminar participants and coaching clients have told me about good and bad leadership characteristics.

A common denominator that has surfaced relative to how leadership has evolved encompasses more of an alignment with the people side of the equation. Professional development and continuous learning also rank high. The people side of the equation can be best described as a heightened awareness about just how valuable every member of the team really is, the "greatest asset" mentality for sure. It also represents some clear linkage to the evolution from Theory X to Theory Y leadership.

Following is a snapshot that captures the leadership evolution perspective of nearly 1000 workshop participants and coaching clients that I've worked with over the past six years.

Good Leadership Characteristics	*Bad Leadership Characteristics*
Lead by example	Blames others
Respectful	Disrespectful
Fairness	Controlling
Integrity	Condescending
Professional	Unethical
Trusts	Dictates
Motivates & Inspires	Takes credit for others work
Knowledgeable - Credible	Micro manages
Empathy – Good listener	Abuses power
Focused – Committed	Untrustworthy
Confident	Plays favoritism
Able to ask for help	Doesn't take responsibility
Consistent	Ambiguous
Demonstrates ownership	No clear plan
Confident & Secure	Close minded
Honest & Trusting	Hostile
Passionate about mission	Rigid
Effective communicator	Inconsistent messages
Visionary	Poor communicator
Ethical	No contingency plan
Enables team success	Loss of human focus
Removes obstacles	"Me first" attitude
Empowers other to lead	Criticizes in public
Develops people	Always right
Teaches	Negative
Shares	Insecure
Encourages new ideas	Authoritarian
Sense of humor	Rude & Abrasive
Fosters teamwork	Lazy
Accepts feedback	Passes the buck
Appreciates	Indecisive

THE EVOLUTION OF LEADERSHIP

From	*To*
Command & Control	Collaborate & Partner
Hierarchical	Cross functional
Dictate	Develop & Navigate
Manage	Lead, Influence & Support
Always right	Willing to admit mistakes
Task orientation	Vision and goals orientation
Bottom line focus	People and culture focus
Head count focus	Right fit focus
Top down influence	Shared influence
Job focus	Career focus
Grow from within	Broader external range
Close minded	Open minded
Rigid	Adaptable-Flexible
Egotistical	Authentic, Caring
Male dominated	More female leaders

Clearly, these represent a narrow view when compared to the millions of American workers who did not provide feedback on the evolution of leadership exercise. It does, however, present some food for thought for all leaders who wish to improve and expand their leadership influence and impact.

As you can see from the above data, a major theme that surfaces is a shift to a kinder and gentler kind of leadership. It is not about weakness, but rather about strength that is born out of leadership authenticity, empathy and respect, each of which have important roots in the deeply important field of Emotional Intelligence, which is often referred to as EI or EQ.

Much has been written about Emotional Intelligence since the mid 1990s when pioneers like Daniel Goleman and Robert Cooper embarked on research and publishing related to EQ. In Daniel Goleman's 1998 landmark book entitled *Working With Emotional Intelligence* (Bantam Books), he states "we are being judged by a new yardstick, not just how smart we are or by our training and expertise but also by how we handle ourselves and each other." At its simplest level, EQ is the combined sum of an individual's social and interpersonal skills. It also encompasses one's ability to sense, understand, and effectively influence other people. The good news is that it is also a skill set or competence that can be learned. An important first step in improving one's EQ is acknowledging that it is in fact very real and deeply connected to what great leaders have in common.

A tremendous resource that supports not only the validity of emotional intelligence but also professional development related to EQ skill building is the EI Consortium. The Consortium represents a global community of both academic researchers and business executives who are committed to the advancement of research and practice related to emotional intelligence in organizations.

In addition to paid membership, The EI Consortium offers a very helpful, no-cost monthly newsletter which can be accessed on line at www.eiconsortium.org.

Building your EQ is also about looking at where you fit within the framework of its core competencies. Robert Cooper in his 1997 book entitled *Executive EQ* (Grosset/ Putnam Publishing) identifies the following as the seven EQ Competencies reflecting a performance edge:

* Emotional self-management
* Leadership agility
* Conscientiousness
* Trustworthiness
* Empathy
* Sensitivity
* Acceptance of diversity

In an effort to help clients take a look at where they fit within the above framework, I created a very simple, non-validated assessment that offers some meaningful insight into development areas related to a few of the key EQ competencies listed above. It should be noted that there are many more extensive and validated assessments available on the market today and that the following is intended to be a first step in your exploration of EQ and its many benefits.

EQ LEADERSHIP SURVEY

For each item listed below, please indicate how well it describes the way you apply EQ in your role as a leader. Circle the number on the rating scale that best represents your style. Five indicates *most* like you while one is *least* like you.

In my role as a leader, I:

1. Let people know when they're doing a good job

    5   4   3   2   1

2. Keep my feelings and emotions in check

    5   4   3   2   1

3. Avoid focusing on people's negative characteristics

    5   4   3   2   1

4. Am willing to admit it when I'm wrong

    5   4   3   2   1

5. Act ethically in my dealings with others

    5   4   3   2   1

6. Can put myself in someone else's shoes

    5   4   3   2   1

7. Look at the bright side of things in and out of work

    5   4   3   2   1

8. Try to focus on people's positive qualities and potential

    5   4   3   2   1

9. Allow my values to guide my daily actions

    5   4   3   2   1

10. Work hard to be a good listener

    5   4   3   2   1

Total Score:

If you scored **40** or more, you are doing a good job of applying some of the key elements of emotional intelligence. If you scored between **30** and **39**, you are well on your way to reaping the benefits of EQ but need to improve your understanding of the process. If you scored less than **30**, this is an important development opportunity for you. Solicit guidance from a trusted colleague or mentor and look for ways to expand your knowledge of EQ and its link to leadership effectiveness.

THE IMPACT OF LOW EQ

Like many senior IT managers, Phil's department experienced a major shift toward outsourcing of IT services at the turn of the century. One of his new outsourcing partners was in India. During the planning stage of his first trip to India, one of his employees proudly informed him that his family lived only a short distance from the city where he would be going. He offered to arrange for his family to meet Phil upon his arrival and even made plans to have his dad show Phil around during his visit. Here was a wonderful opportunity to not only have a local contact in a foreign country, but also a valuable resource as his dad was a well established member of the local business community. Phil took Kavi up on his offer and was off to India.

Shortly after Phil returned, he held a meeting with his staff to update them on his trip. Fairly excited and certainly proud, Kavi inquired about Phil's impressions of India and specifically about his experience with his family. Phil went on for nearly five minutes talking about how much he "hated" his experience in India and how unimpressed he was with nearly every aspect of the trip, the country, its people and most certainly the food. Apparently, Phil had gotten sick on day one and attributed it to the food which he described as "foul." Put yourself in Kavi's shoes for just a minute. This was his country, his family, his culture, his food and he was just trying to help a friend, a colleague. He was so struck by Phil's comments that he left the meeting in tears. I never did find out if Kavi left the company, but my bet would be that if he didn't, he was far less engaged and trusting after Phil's tirade about India than he was before.

There are certainly other examples of low EQ that I've come across in my work over the years, but this one stands out as a powerful one filled with many lessons. What was Phil trying to accomplish with his comments? What good could they possible do? He lacked EQ in a big way. There was no empathy, there was no emotional self-control, no sensitivity, and there was certainly no acceptance of diversity. What a missed opportunity. I'm not advocating that he lie about his trip, I'm strongly advocating that he think first and consider the implications of his comments. In doing so, he would have set a very different course for not just Kavi, but also for his entire staff. You can be sure that the other team members who witnessed Phil's tirade had less trust and respect for him following that staff meeting.

Successful leaders today use more than EQ to help them be effective. However, as referenced earlier, it represents an important part of what great leaders have in common. A good way of building your EQ is to review your answers from the EQ Survey and select at least two areas for your own development. Read any of the many great books on the subject, talk to friends and colleagues, and even consider hiring a leadership coach who can help you with this important and worthwhile task.

BAD LEADERS ARE TEACHERS TOO

We can all learn much about great leadership from our own experiences. There was a time in my career when I thought that the only historical learning opportunity came from my former "good bosses." Thanks to input from a trusted friend and colleague, I expanded my view to believe that we might just be able to learn as much or more from the bad bosses. Think about it, how many of the "bad leadership" characteristics that show up on the previous list have you experienced first hand in your career? How many are worth avoiding at all cost? Make a list for yourself and work to stay connected to it as one of your many leadership guideposts. As you might imagine, doing the same with the "good leadership" characteristics list can be meaningful too. Do it, your team is counting on you!

THANKS FOR THE INSIGHT, RENA

I had just finished a leadership training class with a group of new technical hires at an insurance industry client when Rena approached me with an eager and slightly frustrated look on her face. In my class I had talked about the "golden rule" as a good reminder or guidepost for leaders at any point in their career, including the beginning point. The "golden rule" as I know it is simply, "Treat others the way you want to be treated." Rena was quick to tell me that I had it all wrong. "All wrong?" I asked. What had I missed, I wondered. She went on to tell me that the global workplace of the 21ˢᵗ century required leaders to understand and apply the Platinum Rule. She also went on to tell me that this was a common expectation among her *twentysomething* colleagues. The Platinum Rule as she described it was simply, "Treat others the way *they* want to be treated." I must admit, this made perfect sense to me. After all, how could I possibly expect that what I define as my needs apply to everybody else?

Building clarity around the *what* and the *how* of your team's expectations is not as complicated as it may seem. As a beginning point, I think that this has a lot to do with each team member's individual set of values. Exploring these with your team not only provides tremendous insight, but also demonstrates your capacity to care and hopefully express empathy in the process. In being open to exploring your own evolution as a leader you open up a new world of opportunity to navigate at a higher level, and in the process take your team along for the ride.

Exercises FOR BUILDING
A NAVIGATOR CULTURE

1. Initiate a discussion with your team and even your peer group about how they have seen leadership evolve over their careers. Look for linkage to your leadership strategy and the new realities within your organization.

2. Initiate a discussion with the above groups to develop a list of "good" and "bad" leadership characteristics and then agree to the top five or ten that you and your peer group will encourage (good characteristics) and avoid (bad characteristics).

3. Consider the implications of leadership Theory Y and Theory X within your workgroup and try to expand the foundational guideposts of Theory Y. Consider incorporating these into a statement of your guiding leadership principles.

4. Share the EQ Survey with your peer group and look for ways to support each other's development opportunities. Consider starting an EQ book club within your team or peer group.

5. Solicit feedback from your team on the Platinum Rule concept and ask them to identify the *what* and the *how* of their expectations. Consider a deeper exploration of this by linking it to each person's core values.

Chapter Three

LESSONS FROM THE
NAVIGATOR'S NOTEBOOK

1. Giving or expecting positive feedback when it's warranted is not a bad thing.

2. Wanting employees to work harder is not a bad thing either.

3. Leadership Theory Y is all about the Navigator's path.

4. Clarity and purpose are basic human motivators.

5. People want to be valued and make a difference.

6. Respect, Trust, Integrity and Fairness are key ingredients of great leadership.

7. Emotional Intelligence represents an important part of what great leaders have in common.

8. Most people want to be treated the way *they* want to be treated.

9. Leadership excellence is a journey not a destination.

10. Nobody wants to fail.

The SATISFACTION CONTINUUM

"Everything a leader does or doesn't do impacts
employee satisfaction at some level" —John Honor

Astonished, I repeated my question, do you have any idea how far we live from your location? "Exactly 147 miles" came the reply from the Assistant Manager at Avis Car Rental who went on to explain that his vehicle was equipped with GPS. We had arrived in Newark from Madrid and learned that our connecting flight home had been canceled. Rather than stay the night, we opted to rent a car and drive the final 150 or so miles back to our home in Connecticut. Exhausted from our eight-hour flight and a bit flustered by the canceled connecting flight, we had left a suitcase at the Avis car rental office at Newark airport. Unfortunately, we didn't realize that we had left it behind until we arrived home at 11:30 p.m.

Hoping and praying that we could at least confirm that the missing luggage was still in Newark, I called the rental office. I was also hoping that I would get someone that actually was willing to help or at least demonstrate some level of empathy for our dilemma. Sure enough, the first person I spoke with not only offered empathy, but actually took the time to look for the luggage. To my very pleasant surprise, he came back on the phone after a few minutes and said that he had located the luggage. My huge sense of relief was slightly diminished by the thought that I would now have to change my work schedule the next day so that I could drive some 300+ round trip miles to retrieve the luggage. Not the worst-case scenario by any means, but certainly one that began to fuel my victim emotions. These negative emotions quickly vanished when this very kind person asked if he could deliver the suitcase to our home that evening. Not entirely sure if I had actually heard this offer correctly, I asked him if he knew that we were in Connecticut. He said that he was aware of our location and that he would be happy to deliver the suitcase after he got off work at 12:00 a.m. Astonished, I asked him again if he had any idea how far we lived from his location. It was then that he mentioned the GPS and estimated that he could be at our home by 3:00 a.m. As a further courtesy, he indicated that he would call us when he was ten or fifteen minutes away so that we would not be startled by the door bell when he arrived at our home. In only four hours, our lost luggage nightmare was transformed into a standout example of superior customer service. All because of an employee who cared and who was motivated to really "try harder" to make me feel like a highly valued customer. As you might imagine, Avis has become my only choice for car rentals when away on business or vacation.

Think of the last great customer service experience you had. What happened that made it stand out? More than likely, you'll think of a few really bad experiences before you can get your mind around one that truly stands out as a "wow" experience. How do these wow experiences happen? What are the key actions and behaviors that separate the truly great experiences from those all-too-often bad or negative customer experiences? Even more important, is there a connection to leadership, and if so, what is it? My exploration of these and other related issues began to unfold in a most unexpected way.

Within a few weeks of my Avis car rental experience, I received a call from a long time client who wanted me to do a keynote speech at an upcoming executive conference. When I inquired about the topic of interest for my keynote address, I was informed that the "hot button" issue for this group of thirty or so executives centered on exploring the link between happy employees and happy customers. The big question that resonated among this group was "is there a link," and if so, what can we do as senior leaders to foster this link within our organizations? Fortunately for me, the conference date was four months away and I would have plenty of time to do my research and preparation work. In true Navigator fashion, I began to see the silver lining in my lost luggage experience. If there was a link to be found, it surely was alive and well at Avis in Newark. When I thought about what had created my "wow" experience at Avis, I began to identify all of the ingredients that went into creating this outcome. Empathy, ownership, solution orientation, flexibility, empowerment, customer centeredness, results focused, follow through, and of course a very positive attitude were all part of the equation.

Over the next four months I explored the link between happy employees and happy customers with well over 200 colleagues, clients and friends. I also continued to explore the leadership link that I mentioned above. What I found was not so much surprising as it was powerful in revealing the very obvious. There was a clear link between happy employees and happy customers, and leaders had a great deal to do with this reality. This was the satisfaction continuum. This connection in many ways served as the inspiration for both the title of my keynote address as well as the title of this chapter.

What kind of leader created the empowered, customer-first environment of my lost luggage experience? Which behavioral choice was he or she demonstrating most frequently at work? Despite never meeting this manager, I am very confident that he or she took the Navigator path with a high degree of frequency. Let's start with the strong service orientation that the assistant manager demonstrated. Could that be motivated by a manager who was condescending, abrupt, or overly controlling? Possibly, but very unlikely. Was it created by a manager who was respectful, open, honest, and supportive? More than likely yes. This employee's level of motivation and personal ownership could only be inspired by a manager who takes the Navigator path. Imagine a victim or critic attempting to inspire and motivate employees to create "wow" customer service experiences. I can't. Nor can I imagine a Navigator attempting to inspire mediocrity among his or her team.

THE POWER OF INFLUENCE

Along the way, my research on the employee satisfaction link expanded to encompass a broader look at employee satisfaction and retention. A major theme that I encountered in this process was the idea of leadership influence. At the very core of this discovery is what I have come to define as the *Power of Leadership Influence.* It should be noted that all leaders, and in fact all people, have and use influence in many different ways.

As a beginning point, I have summed up the Leadership Influence concept as having two distinct sides of the equation. When in the *Destructive Influence* mode, leaders are among other things *condescending, evasive, controlling, pessimistic and unrealistic.* By contrast, when they are in the *Productive Influence* mode, they are among other things *respectful, supportive, collaborative, optimistic, and realistic.* Again, another correlation to the four behaviors surfaces. Clearly, the Productive Influence can only come out of the Navigator behavior choice.

Included in my look at retention were some clear business drivers behind maintaining a proactive employee satisfaction process as part of an overall retention strategy. I also explored considerable research on the subject of why employees leave organizations. It has been said by more than a few leadership gurus that the only competitive advantage that successful companies have are their people. Conventional thinking in most organizations today has it that the cost of losing talent and thus the competitive advantage is often a minimum of 100% of the person's salary. The following Retention Strategy Value Proposition worksheet illustrates the numerous costs associated with replacing a key employee. I use this worksheet in many of my consulting assignments and have found it to be a good indicator of the real value associated with employee retention, the foundation of which must include clarity around employee satisfaction drivers. One process that helps clients to define the real business driver behind a proactive retention strategy is to use the worksheet for one of your top employees. Imagine that this "top employee" came into your office tomorrow and much to your surprise informed you that they were leaving. Using the worksheet that follows, do your own assessment of what it would cost to replace this person.

THE RETENTION STRATEGY VALUE PROPOSITION WORK SHEET

Loss & Replacement Costs:

Hiring process costs   =   _____

Separation costs   =   _____

Search Firm fees   =   _____

Training costs   =   _____

Relocation costs   =   _____

Other   =   _____

Business Opportunity Costs:

Loss in productivity costs   =   _____

Overtime costs   =   _____

Contingency workforce costs   =   _____

Loss of customer costs   =   _____

Delay in project or product costs   =   _____

Other   =   _____

Grand Total: =   _____

If you were detailed in your assessment, you were quick to see one of the most significant business drivers related to employee satisfaction. Namely, the substantial amount of time and money that must go into replacing that key employee.

For sure, losing talented employees or for that matter any employee costs time and money. As mentioned earlier, a key building block in the retention strategy must include clarity around employee satisfaction drivers. I have come to believe that assuming that all employees want or like the same thing is a short cut to leadership disaster. If you have a team of ten, you likely have no fewer than five or six key satisfaction drivers among your group. It may also be ten or more. One of the best ways to build clarity around this important issue is to ask your employees for their input either formally through a survey or informally in staff meetings. A good frame of reference that applies here came from my research around the satisfaction drivers. Specifically, it included a look at how employee motivation has evolved over the past thirty or so years. The following is a snapshot of my findings which I have labeled The Evolution of Employee Motivation

THE EVOLUTION OF EMPLOYEE MOTIVATION

1970s	✳	Job Security, Stability
1980s	✳	Money, Perks
1990s	✳	Leisure Time, Flexibility
2000s	✳	Balance, Learning, Recognition
2010s	✳	Values Alignment

If you were one of those people who, like myself, started their career in the 70s, you will quickly relate to the shift from the 70s to the 80s. Having and keeping a job was a very real motivation for most people in the 70s. That's not to say that it isn't a key motivator for most people today, but there has clearly been a shift. In the high flying 80s many employees wanted and expected to make lots of money and certainly the perks that went with the job. Surely many people made lots of money in the 80s, but by the early 90s many people wanted time to enjoy the fruits of their labor. Add to this the massive restructuring of corporate America and it's no wonder that so many people I spoke with had experienced this shift first hand.

Like most significant life events, the turn of the century brought about a higher than normal need for personal reflection. A new millennium, a new beginning, *What am I doing this for? What do I want from all of this?* were just some of the reflections that people I spoke with remembered. My experience with these personal reflections at the turn of the century created a real thirst for the truth and a strong desire to make sense of things. I had been like many leaders at the time, running faster and faster constantly trying to do more with less and of course feeling a bit overwhelmed. A major and very powerful byproduct of the personal reflection was the heightened awareness about personal values. Back to the basic questions of *Why am I here* and *What do I want from all of this?* One colleague summed it up quite nicely by saying that "I expect to have to work for the next twenty years or so, and I refuse to have it be a bad experience."

Following the turn of the century, many folks seemed to share my thinking about the values alignment as well as the desire to be more fully recognized for their efforts. Unfortunately for many people, the increasing demands of our fast-paced work environment prevent them from getting positive feedback more often than once a year during the obligatory "annual review." Like many folks I spoke with, this once-a-year event is often light on positive feedback and heavy on "let's get through this"—the old "check-it-off-the-list" style of leadership that is unfortunately more common than most of us want to believe.

Another positive link to the values alignment shift is the heightened awareness around why employees leave organizations. As you might imagine or even know first hand, money is no longer the main reason why folks stay at companies for ten or twenty or even thirty years. Sure, it's a factor, but more times than not it's low on the list. As I began the last stages of my keynote address preparation, I was compelled to dig deeper into the issue of why folks leave their companies. A lot has been written on this subject, and the debate continues to rage in many Human Resource circles. The question of "why are we losing our talent" is and should be a front and center issue in all HR circles. Marcus Buckingham in his groundbreaking 1999 book entitled *First Break All of the Rules* (Simon & Shuster Publishing), summed up the debate and for the new reality quite well when he said, "People don't leave companies, they leave managers." His extensive national research into this key business challenge helped open the eyes of many leaders both in and out of Human Resources.

Intrigued by Buckingham's work, I conducted my own informal research to uncover what I could about why folks leave organizations. I spoke with over one hundred friends and colleagues to gain their perspective on this issue. What I found ran parallel to not only Bucking-ham's work, but also my own inner instincts about the subject. Again and again, I heard that money was not the issue and that the idea of leaving your manager and not the company was very real. The following is a summary of what I uncovered through my informal research on the subject of why folks leave companies or managers.

EXPLORING WHY EMPLOYEES LEAVE

* Bad or dysfunctional leadership
* Values and needs not in sync with organization
* Don't feel recognized or valued
* Lack of job, role, or organizational clarity
* Limited or non existent career path
* Lack of learning and development options

While all of the above are linked to employee moti-vation and satisfaction at one level or another, the com-mon thread that runs throughout is the values alignment issue. It may be different for every member of your team, but that doesn't diminish the opportunity you have as a leader to improve employee satisfaction and retention along the Navigator path.

My Satisfaction Continuum keynote address went very well. There was an abundance of good dialogue and consensus around the opportunities that leaders have to create employee satisfaction every day. One of the exec-utives in attendance expressed his curiosity around the issue of developing no costs or low costs strategies for improving employee satisfaction and engagement. A new frontier for my informal research efforts, I thought. Over the next month I assembled the following list, which was compiled through the kind efforts of many colleagues.

One of my favorites is the "five pennies" strategy, which I will discuss following the list.

LOW COST–LOW MAINTENANCE EMPLOYEE SATISFACTION TIPS

* Establish an employee retention task force
* Solicit feedback on what employees want
* Allow job sharing & flex time if possible
* Establish informal career management clubs
* Create an Employee Hall Of Fame
* Have key leaders send thank you notes monthly
* Take one star performer to lunch each month
* Create a "fun" suggestion box
* Actively seek out star performers–solicit their help
* Find ways to communicate success stories
* Offer "dress up" Monday's
* Do one "fun" staff meeting per month
* Give movie tickets as a way of saying thank you
* Utilize "five pennies" recognition strategy

The five penny recognition strategy worked well on me. I had just been promoted to my first leadership role, and, knowing that I needed help, I called one of my first bosses for guidance. I explained that I needed a few of his leadership gems of wisdom to help me on my way to becoming a real leader. His first gem was the "five pennies" strategy, which he said worked well on me and several of my former co-workers. He went on to tell me that good leadership had a lot to do with making people feel valued. He also said that even well intentioned leaders forget this some times; hence the five penny strategy. Every day before he left his home for work, he would place five pennies in his left pants pocket. One of his leadership goals for every day was to say something positive to at least five people on his team. Every time he did, he would move one penny to the right pant pocket. He told me that he knew he had done something important every day when he arrived home with five pennies in his right hand pocket. It sure is simple when you think about it, but it is also very powerful. Could you and your team benefit from the five pennies strategy? There are many excellent resources for other low cost, low maintenance employee satisfaction tips. One of my favorites is Bob Nelson's 1001 *Ways To Reward Employees* (Workman Publishing). Bob even offers a free weekly newsletter via his web site (nelson-motivation.com), which is chock full of ideas and guidance on the subject.

There is a clear link between happy employees and happy customers, and that link is *you*. You as the leader are the bridge that allows the satisfaction continuum to exist. Sure there are challenges, shifting priorities and competing expectations, but you are the Navigator, you hold the compass. The shift to values alignment as a form of employee motivation represents a fabulous opportunity to build the connection between work and a higher purpose. Only through clarity and navigational leadership can you expect your team to discover their greater purpose at work and the common ground they share. I firmly believe that absent this deeper and more meaningful connection, the "white water" pace of today's work environment will leave many casualties in its wake.

Group Activities FOR BUILDING A NAVIGATOR CULTURE

1. Ask your team and/or leadership peer group to define the leadership characteristics or behaviors that help create a "wow" customer experience. Further explore the daily or weekly measures that can be linked to these characteristics or behaviors.

2. Initiate discussion with direct reports regarding their perception of employee satisfaction within your area. If applicable, employee survey data could be a good baseline to work from.

3. Initiate discussion with direct reports regarding their thoughts on the concept of Leadership Influence and specifically Productive and Destructive influence.

4. Incorporate discussion of the Low Cost-Low Maintenance Tips in staff meetings to help identify team preferences and possible additions to the list.

5. Solicit feedback from direct reports and peer groups regarding their role in retaining key employees. Also identify key leadership actions that support this process.

Chapter Four

LESSONS FROM THE
NAVIGATOR'S NOTEBOOK

---

1. Great leadership is the link between happy employees and happy customers.

2. Productive influence embodies the Navigator path.

3. Destructive influence is the opposite of power.

4. People don't leave companies, they leave managers.

5. Everybody likes a compliment.

6. Employee motivation has evolved.

7. A common thread that runs through employee motivation is values alignment.

8. The five pennies strategy works.

9. Values alignment represents a fabulous opportunity to create a connection between work and a higher purpose.

10. You hold the compass.

The LEADER as a COACH

"The purpose of the leader is to create more leaders and less followers"—John Iacobelli

One of my all-time favorite Dilbert cartoons features the fictional character Alice who is instructed by her "pointy haired" boss to write a performance review of herself for him to sign. Alice asks, "What will our seven layers of management be doing while I manage myself?" Responding to the angry look on her boss's face, she adds "Sorry, I'll ding myself for that on my evaluation." Her boss then replies, "If you can't find me, have Carol my secretary sign my name."

What just happened here and just how often is this error in leadership judgment played out in the offices and cubicles of Corporate America? *Too often* is likely the correct answer. While there is certainly some humor to be found in this and for that matter most Dilbert cartoons, there is nothing funny about skirting one of your most critical leadership responsibilities, namely employee development discussions. All too often these discussions get relegated to the dreaded once-a-year routine where very little benefit actually occurs. I remember a recent coaching case where in the early project assessment phase the HR Head told me that "Bob's issue had been going on for nearly three years." When I asked the usual question about Bob's perception of "the issue," I was told that he didn't have a clue because no one had ever told him about "the issue." This may come as a surprise to you, but I have seen this scenario play out more times than I care to remember. How could this be? I know, I've asked that question, too. The real shocker in many of these cases is that not only does the person not get to hear about the "issue"; they go on getting average or above average performance ratings and even bonuses despite the fact that their behavior or lack of results is creating "an issue."

One of the reasons that the above scenario plays out with a high degree of frequency is that many leaders view the whole idea of employee coaching and development as a very complex and time-consuming process. It's not, or at least it doesn't have to be. Getting one's arms around the idea of employee coaching and development begins with acknowledging that this is a critical part of good leadership. It also helps to understand that good leadership is among other things about creating more leaders to carry the torch. Another reality today is that many world class organizations now have clearly defined performance metrics for their leaders that are linked to employee development. Regardless of the motivation, it makes good business sense for leaders to develop real and meaningful strategies for developing their own coaching capacity as part of their overall leadership focus. It is also helpful to create a context for better understanding what coaching is and what it is not. The following is a good frame of reference to consider.

Coaching is not: Psychotherapy, Limited to poor performers, Complicated, Optional.

Coaching is: Open and timely dialogue, Honest & respectful, Success oriented, Ongoing.

Often times, leaders get distracted by the misconception that they need to be therapists or counselors when it comes to employee coaching and development. They do not. What they often need to be more of is open and honest and clearly supportive of the person's success. It also helps to recognize that all employees have development needs, not just the poor performers.

There are many areas or scenarios in which a coaching discussion is relevant. Some potential examples include Personal Enrichment, Professional Development, Performance Improvement and Career Advancement. In the Personal Enrichment scenario the employee may want to expand his or her knowledge of an area that will help them in their role in a non-direct way. It may be learning a new language or even taking a course related to a hobby. In both the Professional Development and Performance Improvement scenarios, it is more than likely related to helping them to expand their impact in their job. The Career Advancement scenario often is linked to their long-term career goals beyond their current role. Regardless of the scenario, it is important to have and follow a process that moves the employee in the right direction. It's also important to remember that all of the above scenarios encompass learning and learning is good.

The following is a five step process that I have used with many leaders who wish to expand their capacity to coach and develop their employees.

Step #1: Identify the issue—*what, why, how* and *when* questions must be included

Step #2: Establish agreement that the issue exists and has consequences if applicable

Step #3: Explore and define appropriate solutions, related actions and metrics

Step #4: Provide follow-up support and monitor progress

Step #5: Acknowledge progress and success

While there are many other very effective coaching processes that you can follow, the above represents a rather straight-forward process for helping to make sense of your employee coaching leadership responsibility. More importantly, it provides a workable framework for achieving a higher level of employee productivity.

Within this coaching process, there are some key considerations that must be addressed to ensure success. As a beginning point, it is important to select the right employee for your coaching activity, the *Who* of the coaching equation. Targeting success from the onset is a good place to begin. Considering the employee's history with handling feedback well and demonstrating an above average level of personal ownership are all factors that will influence a positive outcome. Seeking clarity and consensus around the actual development need is of course critical.

The probability of long-term success is greatly diminished absent a high degree of clarity around the *What* of the coaching equation. Linked to the *What* of the coaching equation is the *Why.* Including discussion about the issues impact, value of action and desired outcomes including benefits goes a long way in helping the employee move forward. Defining the desired plan of action, the *How* of the coaching equation is also key. The *How* may include specific training, periodic feedback, observation and other targeted learning opportunities. Finally, the *When* of the coaching equation helps bring the action plan to life by providing specific short and long-term milestones that serve to build momentum and overall coaching success.

Beyond following the above format, it helps to understand some other important ingredients that serve to ensure a positive outcome. These include but are not limited to Trust, Respect, Honesty, Support, Ownership and Confidentiality. They are all at one level or another self-evident. However, the power of Trust can not be overestimated or down played. Absent trust in your character, intentions, and overall support, the employee will at best be suspect of your coaching agenda. At worst, they may just decide to leave for fear that they are "marked" and that their future on your team is limited. In one of my leadership development classes some years ago I initiated a discussion with the group about the power of trust and specifically about what went into to building trust as a leader. The following came to be called the Leadership Trust Inventory. As you will see, it is really a series of statements that great leaders affirm not just in their own minds but more importantly in their daily actions.

THE LEADERSHIP TRUST INVENTORY

* I follow through on my commitments
* I encourage feedback
* I admit my own mistakes
* I treat all employees fairly
* I promote honest and open communication
* I confront when necessary
* I openly value and encourage other perspectives

* I consistently act in an ethical manner
* I never contribute to the "rumor mill"
* I am a positive role model for my team

Of course, all of this begs the question, what's your trust profile? If it's not as high as you'd like, pick the areas above that you can work on and commit to building your trust profile among your team.

As you can see, the employee coaching process is not overly complicated. When you have a meaningful plan, it can be a very straight forward process that helps you increase the productivity of each and every member of your team. While all of what we have covered so far is centered on how to make the coaching process work well, it is important to look at how and why it can fail. Coaching fails when you:

* Assume that the person understands the issue
* Talk in generalities and not specifics
* Don't get the person involved in identifying and owning the solution
* Focus on attitude instead of behavior
* Only focus on the negative aspects of the person's work
* Don't have a plan for monitoring progress
* Assume that success comes in short order
* Don't provide positive reinforcement

"Giving timely and specific feedback is the quickest, cheapest and most cost effective intervention for improving employee performance." Ferdinand Fournier from his book *Coaching For Improved Work Performance*, (McGraw Hill Publishing).

The power and value of timely feedback can not be overstated. As a beginning point, it helps to minimize ambiguity, keeps employees focused and serves to expand your leadership influence. It is also another important common denominator of great leaders.

Choosing the right type of feedback is another important consideration. Like our earlier review of my leadership influence concept, feedback can take the form of Productive or Destructive. It can also take the form of Neutral. Often the destructive form of feedback has it roots in the victim or critic leadership behavioral mode. It is likely connected to the *reactive* versus *relating* mode of thinking. In the Destructive context the feedback typically creates a negative tone that puts the employee on the defensive. Some examples of Destructive feedback that clients have shared with me include;

* What's wrong with you?
* Your attitude stinks!
* I'm getting really tired of your _____
* You always drop the ball
* I just can't handle this anymore
* You never _____

As you can see, none of the above helps to engage the employee in a meaningful or solution-oriented way. Granted, there are times when your employee's bad behavior or lack of results has you at the end of your leadership rope. You just want to scream. Despite your best efforts, they don't seem to get it and they can't seem to come around. Be careful—some employees may never get it. You have to draw the line at some point because diverting all of your energy and attention away from the good or superior employees can have a cost. Often this cost manifests itself in reduced morale and employee engagement because your star performers end up feeling neglected. They may not need the same level of attention that your under-performers need, but they still need your attention.

Abraham Lincoln once said that "everyone likes a compliment now and then." I know I do and I suspect that every one on your team does, too. Productive feedback should be genuine, real, and specific. Like all three types of feedback, it should also be timely. Waiting a few days or even a few weeks to provide any type of feedback diminishes the value and impact of it. Waiting until the annual review, as you might imagine, is the worst case scenario. Unfortunately, I think this happens in far too many organizations today.

Productive feedback lets employees know that they matter, that they are appreciated and that their opinion and input counts for something. Some examples of Productive feedback that I have heard about or used include:

* Thanks for your extra effort
* That was a good point you made in the meeting today
* I was counting on you and you didn't let me down
* I'm glad that you're part of the team
* We couldn't have done it without you
* You're a great role model for the team
* You are well on your way to being a super star in our company

Notice the last example. Unlike the others, it sets the tone for a development discussion. On one hand the person is clearly successful as they are "well on their way" but also not quite there yet. Here in lies a wonderful coaching opportunity, an opportunity to help that employee take their performance to the next level, with your help.

Providing Neutral feedback is by far a more effective way of dealing with performance-type issues. Unlike the Destructive feedback scenario, the Neutral feedback scenario allows the employee to participate in not only the discovery process, but perhaps more importantly the solutions-generation process. In this scenario, the employee is not put on the defensive but rather is encouraged to explore the opportunity or upside of the performance improvement issue. Some examples of Neutral feedback include:

* Help me understand why you did
* Do you know that you frequently?
* Are you aware that you?
* Do you know that this is the 3rd time we've talked about?
* Tell me about
* I've noticed that sometimes you
* How can I help you with?

As you can see, the Neutral feedback scenario allows the employee to more fully participate in the coaching and performance discussion. It also helps to build clarity around the performance issue while allowing them to be part of the solution. Regardless of which Neutral or Productive feedback option you choose, it is important to follow a plan and be well prepared. Part of the coaching plan can and should include actions that you can take to expand your capacity to effectively coach your team. The following Coaching Effectiveness Survey is a helpful tool for gaining insight into your own development opportunities as they relate to being an effective coach.

COACHING EFFECTIVENESS SURVEY

For each item listed below, please indicate how well it describes the way you "Coach" in your role as a leader. Circle the number on the rating scale that best represents your coaching style. Five indicates *most* like you while one is *least* like you.

In my role as a leader, I:

1. Help employees identify development opportunities
   5   4   3   2   1
2. Am comfortable providing constructive feedback
   5   4   3   2   1
3. Avoid being judgmental or overly critical
   5   4   3   2   1
4. Help employees set attainable goals
   5   4   3   2   1
5. Have a plan for monitoring progress
   5   4   3   2   1
6. Demonstrate respect for each person's contribution
   5   4   3   2   1
7. Maintain confidentiality with development needs
   5   4   3   2   1
8. Work to create an environment of trust
   5   4   3   2   1
9. Try to remove barriers to success
   5   4   3   2   1
10. Am a role model for my team
    5   4   3   2   1

Total Score:

If you scored 40 or more, you are doing a good job of applying many of the key actions of an effective coach. If you scored between 30 and 39, you are well on your way to helping your team maximize their full potential but need to improve your understanding of the process. If you scored less than 30, this is an important development opportunity for you. Solicit guidance from a trusted colleague or mentor and look for ways to expand your knowledge of coaching and employee development. Your team is counting on you!

It has been said that one of the most important building blocks of great leaders is their acknowledgment that they can always get better. Coaching and employee development is no exception. Review your total score from the Coaching Effectiveness Survey and select the two or three lowest ranked items as part of your own development plan. You can get better at this and it's not overly complicated. Commit to working on at least one of the areas, and in time you and your team will see a positive difference.

Another way that you can improve your coaching effectiveness capacity is to actually get out of your office and do it. Stop the busy work, stop the distractions. You have people on your team right now that are ready to be coached. You just need to take the first step. It also helps to have a meaningful game plan. As you might imagine, coaching and employee development is not a guessing game and it's certainly not something you can afford to improvise. The following Coaching Game Plan was developed several years ago as part of one of my leadership classes. It can serve as an important framework for not just helping to develop your people but also to measure your own coaching capacity.

YOUR COACHING GAME PLAN

Use this worksheet to think about a current performance issue that you have with one of your people and to develop a plan for applying the lessons from this chapter. Refer to your plan during your meeting with the employee to help ensure that you stay on the right track.

Employee:
Target date for discussion:
Describe the issue that exists:

_____

_____

_____

What are some concrete examples that will illustrate the issue?

_____

_____

_____

Step One: Get agreement that the issue exists

* What questions will you ask?
* How will the employee respond to your feedback?
* How can you modify your approach to ensure trust and consensus?

* What did you agree to as the key issue and opportunity?

Step Two: Define your solution

* What are the alternatives?
* What is the most "doable" and meaningful solution?
* What is the time line for implementing the solution?
* What does success look like? How will it be measured?

Step Three: Follow-up

* When will you follow-up?
* Are there barriers to success that you can help remove?

Step Four: Acknowledge Success

* How will you recognize progress and success?
* What can you do to build on this success and avoid a repeat of the issue?

Notes to myself:

_____

_____

_____

_____

_____

As mentioned earlier, it makes good sense to target success when selecting the employee who you will coach, especially as you work to build your coaching skills. Success breeds success, as the saying goes. It also makes sense to incorporate a bit of your own style or voice into the above coaching game plan as well as the overall coaching process. Bringing your voice to the equation allows for a more real and potentially more meaningful coaching partnership that helps foster development on both sides of the coaching equation.

Exercises FOR BUILDING
A NAVIGATOR CULTURE

1. Initiate a discussion with your leadership peer group about their views and experiences related to employee coaching and development and look to expand your own coaching framework using this chapter as your guide.

2. Seek out your HR team for help with the coaching process and work to engage them as your partners in employee development.

3. Identify your bottom three performers and explore what can be done in a collaborative way to help improve their standing through a coaching intervention.

4. Create a coaching development book club within your team and/or peer group and look for ways to build the coaching capacity of multiple people in your organization.

5. Identify one key employee who would benefit from a coaching and development discussion and who would allow you to build on your coaching capacity. Remember to target success especially with the first few employees you coach.

Chapter Five

LESSONS FROM THE
NAVIGATOR'S NOTEBOOK

---

1. Leadership is in some ways about creating more leaders.

2. You can not delegate your leadership responsibilities.

3. Choosing to ignore the coaching "issue" serves no one's best interest.

4. Employee coaching is not complicated and it's not limited to poor performers.

5. The power of trust can not be overestimated.

6. Lack of clarity is a major impediment to coaching success.

7. Feedback should always be specific and timely.

8. The Leadership Influence concept applies to employee coaching too.

9. Diverting your energy and attention away from star performers may cost you.

10. Everybody likes a compliment now and then.

SAILING *the* WINDS
of CHANGE

*"It is not the strongest of the species that
survive, nor the most intelligent, but the one
most responsive to change"* —*Charles Darwin*

I n early 2003, I had the good fortune of leaving behind
the cold and snowy weather of New England for a
three-day consulting assignment in Tampa, Florida.
My work on this assignment involved doing six half-day
training classes on the subject of organizational change
for a subsidiary of one of my Hartford-based clients. One
of the first things that struck me on day one of the project
was the abundance of palm trees just outside my training
room window. The seventy-five-degree, sunny weather
also caught my attention. Granted, this was probably the
norm for most upscale office parks in Tampa and other
metropolitan cities in Florida. As a life long resident of
the Northeast, I must admit that seeing palm tress out
side my window was something that I instinctively associated with a vacation experience, not a work experience.

The training classes went well, all or at least most of
the participants were engaged and the senior site manager seemed very pleased with how things had gone.
"This was just what we needed," she beamed as I left for

the airport on day four. At some point during my forty-five-minute cab ride, the thought occurred to me that I had just witnessed another major discovery related to the four behaviors. Sure there was the usual mix of the four behavior types in my six classes and of course the critics were most vocal, but there was one unexpected learning that really stood out. The extent that employees will go to in feeding and embellishing the rumor mill, especially as it relates to organizational change, is really pretty amazing.

In chapter one, I briefly referenced the "department of employee complication," which I used as an illustration of the victim and critic behavioral mind set. During my change management classes in Tampa, I had helped the group uncover the usual range of issues that were driving change in their workplace. Technology, Market Competition, Government Regulations, Shareholder Value, all of these were at play. What I hadn't factored in was the department of employee complication. During one of my routine exercises in the change management workshop, I asked the participants to define the reasons or drivers behind the change issues that they had identified in an earlier exercise. Yes, they did identify the ones listed here, but they also identified the department of employee complication as a major force of change. Puzzled, I inquired about this assessment.

Remember, these folks were 1000 miles away from corporate headquarters. A corporate headquarters that was well known for its many elegant and elaborate furnishings, including original works of art. It was a stately building with multiple floors in one of the most desirable sections of the city. It had terraces and gardens on the top floor, which not surprisingly was where the top executives made their offices. The Tampa employees went on to tell me that they were quite sure that these same executives, "feeling a bit envious of the great Florida weather," sat around on their garden terraces and plotted how to make the lives of those "pee-ons" in Tampa miserable. Pretty wild idea indeed, I thought. When I dug deeper, I was quick to understand that this whole idea of the sinister plot at corporate headquarters was clearly being driven by the critics and victims of the group. It was on many levels the foundation of their rumor mill. All six classes shared the same story almost with the same level of detail and certainly the same level of conviction. Like many organizations today, the rumor mill was alive and well, or not so well.

The rumor mill can be a very powerful force to reckon with for leaders at any time, but especially difficult during times of change. The truth is that the rumor mill is never positive. You'll never hear a rumor about how great things are or about how much people like the boss. Often times it's filled with venom—nasty half truths at best that all serve to distract the team from the job at hand. At its worst level, the rumor mill saps the energy of the group and can lead to actual sabotage of key initiatives. Sounds strong, but believe me, it happens.

As mentioned in Chapter One, the critics and victims thrive on building communities of believers. This I think gives them strength, although ironically these behaviors do the reverse. It also helps to validate their distorted view of things, especially their work and their leader's agenda. While it's next to impossible to completely eradicate the rumor mill from corporate life today, there are many things that a leader can do to minimize its impact. We'll take a closer look at this in the next chapter, but for now suffice to say that communication, lots of communication is a major part of the solution equation.

Creating a context for change is a good starting point in helping employees understand the realities of their work environment, including your new and possibly expanded expectations of them. Max DePree in his **1989** book entitled *Leadership Is An Art* (Dell Publishing) states among other things that "the first responsibility of a leader is to define reality." Funny how simple and obvious that seems, but the truth of the matter is that "reality" is subjective. My reality may be very different from yours and so goes the scenario if you have a team of two or twenty-two. Business or work reality at its very foundation has a lot to do with how things are new, different or evolving. Putting this in the context of what is expected for each employee and for your department or division helps avoid ambiguity and greatly slows or inhibits the rumor mill.

The reality element is also about defining the forces of change, those internal and external factors that drive the change. Not surprisingly, most of the significant change experienced by organizations today is external in nature. Sure there are internal factors, but external factors like globalization, competition, technology, and shifting demographics are critical forces that all organizations must deal with and respond to in order to survive or thrive. So often these external forces are the drivers of the internal forces. These external forces create a ripple affect that transcends the entire organizational structure. Consider the following example;

Patriot Manufacturing founded in **1972** has a proud history of producing high-quality fabrics that are used in aerospace and military applications. They have maintained a steady increase in sales and revenue over the past twelve years. By all accounts, they are a very successful business. Like many American manufacturers, Patriot has seen its share of foreign competition. In fact, only twenty years ago they were one of just five U.S. suppliers that competed in their marketplace, which was largely domestic in scale. Today the number is nearly twenty-five, half of which are foreign manufacturing concerns. This increased competition (an external force) has required them to implement many new cost savings and quality initiatives just to stay competitive. From new manufacturing and marketing strategies to the way that billing gets done, this one external factor has created significant changes for everyone at Patriot. Included in this equation is the technology element of change, which is another external force. No longer can Patriot afford to use cutting and packaging machinery that met the needs of the pre-globalization marketplace. Today, they operate with the much more sophisticated numerically controlled machinery, and nearly one third of their production cycle is fully automated. The way most employees of Patriot did their jobs even a few years ago is very different today. Creating a context for helping them to understand these changes is a huge and critical responsibility of the leadership team at Patriot.

In building clarity around the "reality-based" context of change, leaders help to remove what I call the "personal context" of change. This personal context often serves as the fuel that not only feeds the rumor mill but also fosters an atmosphere of victims and critics. Like my earlier example of the department of employee complication, the personal context of change stems from a belief system that is rooted in an "us *versus* them" mentality. This personal context involves taking the change and its associated shift in job focus *personally*, almost as if it's someone else's fault. I have seen more than a few successful people over the years allow this flawed thinking to adversely impact their reputation and standing in their organizations. Despite the deeply rooted beliefs of the victims and critics, most organizational change stems from external factors that require the organization to adapt or seriously jeopardize their future.

As much as the personal context of change may seem to be more emotionally driven than fact driven, it should not be ignored. Understanding the people side of the change equation is critical. There has been much written over the years about the various stages of human transition during change, and all of it serves a purpose. Regardless of which model or philosophy you subscribe to, it's safe to say that everyone deals with change differently. In the early stages of change most people will be in what is commonly called the denial stage. In this stage (and for any number of reasons), the person uses denial to guard against the pending doom. "It's not happening, and it will go away if I just ignore it." Following the denial stage, most people experience some level of resistance. That is they push back and may even cling to the past hoping that things will return to the "good old days." After hours or days or even months, most employees shift into the acceptance stage, or what I like to call the exploration stage. In this stage they begin to see the opportunity. They are reminded of how they've gotten through similar obstacles and are hopeful as a result. Finally, people tend to move into the commitment stage where they are "on board" and moving in the right direction. I think it is important to note that everyone experiences these stages differently and certainly over very different time frames.

Beyond some insight into the various transition stages, it is important to understand some of the issues that impact the length of each stage of the change transition period. Leadership, both good and bad, is a big factor. So is the sense of loss that people typically experience while in the change transition. During change good leaders listen and communicate frequently. They also tend to identify and seek out team members who are struggling and in turn offer help and support through the stages of change transition.

If ever your team needs good leadership, it is certainly during times of change. Understanding and responding to the sense of loss that your team might feel during the change transition period is very important. Some of the common feelings of loss that employees experience during times of change include:

* Loss of Attachment
* Loss of Turf
* Loss of Structure
* Loss of an Understood or Expected Future
* Loss of Meaning
* Loss of Control

Again, like the varying durations of each stage of change transition, the sense of loss and its impact is different for everybody. Encouraging your team to explore this and to be open to helping each other can go a long way in allowing your team to come out of the change transition curve faster and in a more cohesive manner.

Supporting your team during change goes well

beyond helping them through the change transition period. In many ways it encompasses being the change agent that models the desired attitudes and behaviors. Sure, leadership at many levels is about being a positive role model, but it's even more relevant when the winds of change are at gale force. There are many ways to define a change agent and even more ways to describe what they do. I have my theory on all of this, and in true Navigator fashion I like to keep it simple. Some of the important change agent competencies that come to mind include:

* Flexible
* Risk Tolerant
* Innovative–Creative
* Stress Tolerant
* Optimistic

Another part of being the leader role model, especially during times of change, is to assess how you deal with change both as a leader-influencer and as an individual member of the larger organization. Like all aspects of great leadership, there is always room for improvement. An effective way of measuring your response to change specifically as a leader involves taking stock of the many important leadership actions that go into leading people during change. The following Change Leadership Inventory offers some good insight into these actions along with a measure of where you fit in the change leadership equation. Review your answers and identify one or two of your best development opportunities related to leading your team through change. Any meaningful action is sure to help your team stay focused and moving in the right direction.

CHANGE MANAGEMENT
LEADERSHIP INVENTORY

Answer the following questions regarding your change management leadership skills as honestly and objectively as possible. Circle the number on the rating scale that best represents your style. Five indicates *most* like you while one is *least* like you.

When I am called upon to implement change, I:

1. Give my direct reports as much advance notice as possible

    5   4   3   2   1

2. Explain the change as completely as possible

    5   4   3   2   1

3. Avoid making changes that are not critical

    5   4   3   2   1

4. Provide change specific training opportunities

    5   4   3   2   1

5. Hold each person accountable for some element of change

    5   4   3   2   1

6. Provide assistance to those who find it difficult to change

    5   4   3   2   1

7. Encourage people to think and act "out of the box"

    5   4   3   2   1

8. Look for the positive in the change initiative

    5   4   3   2   1

9. Celebrate even small success as progress is made

    5   4   3   2   1

10. Model the desired behaviors and attitude

    5   4   3   2   1

Total Score:

If you scored 40 or more, you are a master of organizational change and transformation. If you scored between 30 and 39, you are well on your way to being a change agent but need to improve your understanding of the process. If you scored less than 30, this is an important development opportunity for you. Try to become a student of the change process and look for opportunities to model the desired behaviors of a change agent. Your team is counting on you.

As I'm sure you noticed a common denominator of the Change Management Leadership Inventory is communication. I mentioned earlier that communication, lots of communication, is a good way of minimizing the rumor mill and its associated fallout. It is also a good way to reduce the stress and anxiety related to change. Humor is another way.

Several years ago a colleague gave me a very insightful and humorous book entitled *Change- Busting, 50 Ways to Sabotage Organization Change* by Carol Kinsey Goman (KCS Publishing). This book is especially interesting because it uses cartoons to illustrate ways in which people can and do sabotage progress during times of change.

While all of the cartoons in the book are on the mark, my favorite involves a picture of a huge electronics control console, like something you would see at a NASA control center, ten feet high and ten feet wide with no less than a thousand dials, gauges, and switches. Standing next to this huge, very intimidating technical monstrosity are two people. One is holding the cord to the control panel console and the other stands almost frozen, with a very puzzled look on his face. The caption reads, *here's the plug, anything else you need to know?*

The leadership parallel in my mind is the leader who

announces that "we all need to change, so let's get on with it." "Hurry up, get on the bus, we're moving forward." No time for understanding, no time for the road map and certainly no time for identifying the "what" of the change, the new direction, and of course the new expectations.

The *what* of change represents a very important part of the leadership communication strategy that must be in place during the change process. There are of course other elements, which we will examine here.

I delivered my first change management training class nearly a dozen years ago and have delivered well over one hundred since that time. I have also had countless discussions about the perils of change with various clients and colleagues over this same period. One thing that stands out from all of these experiences is the critical need of all leaders to communicate in a clear and consistent fashion. This is such a complex issue that I have devoted the following chapter to the subject. For now, however, we will explore the leadership communication scenario as it relates to organizational change.

A good illustration of the need for consistent communication from all leaders is what I call the "lunch room" scenario. Imagine for a moment that I showed up for lunch at your company and randomly picked a table with six employees. I asked them to identify the biggest changes at your company and in their work and then asked them to identify the organizational response to these changes. Would everyone tell the same story? Would everyone be clear on the *what* and *why* of the change? Even more importantly, would they all understand their role in supporting the change? Chances are, your answers made you lose your appetite for lunch all together. The truth is that in most organizations today, I would hear some very different stories, most of which had a stronger connection to the rumor mill than they did the new realities of your organization or industry.

Beyond the *What* of a change communication strategy is the Why, How and When of change. The *what* of change is best summed up by the very simple question: What's happening? Linking the external and internal change factors or forces of change must be included in the *what* part of the equation. They are also in most cases the direct link to the why of the change, and as such need to be part of the change communication equation.

Finally, the *How* and *When* of the change communication strategy allows you to set the actual course by defining how the team or organization is going to get there and when they should leave and arrive at whatever the new organizational destination looks like. Because of the critical importance of having a consistent message during times of change, I have listed below the key components that encompass an effective change leadership communication strategy.

* **The What** answers the question "What's happening?"
* **The Why** answers the question "Why is this happening to us?"
* **The How** answers the question "How do we all need to respond?"
* **The Where** answers the question "Where are we going?"
* **The When** answers the questions "When do we begin?" and "When do we get there?"

As you might imagine, none of this can be over communicated. The more often people hear consistent answers to these questions, the more you have done to help them come out of the change transition cycle better off and certainly more engaged.

My last employer had just been acquired by a European firm, and everything changed very quickly. Key people left, new systems and processes were implemented, and the success you created yesterday didn't seem to matter much. The new focus was clearly on bottom line results today. Not that we didn't produce good bottom line results each quarter, we did, but the new parent company just wanted more, lots more. As someone who lives and breathes business, I clearly understand this. I don't even have a problem with it. Heck, if you or I had written the check for the acquisition, we'd want a good return on our investment, too. The issue for me was less at the business level and more at the personal level. Frankly, I struggled with the rapid fire changes and some days felt that they didn't make much sense. Still, I navigated along as best I could, or least I thought I did.

One day several months after the acquisition, a dear friend asked me how I was doing with all of the changes. She sensed that I was struggling. I confessed that I was and told her that I was reaching my change saturation point, a point I believe we all have and one that ultimately leads to burnout if we don't deal with it in a constructive way. She really got my attention when she asked how my team was doing especially in view of how I was doing. I must admit that this question was a big wake-up call for me, largely because everything I did was about my team. I was lucky to have some of the best people in my industry on my team and I knew it. They created my

success in a big way. They inspired me more than I think
I inspired them. Had I let them down by not being more
of a Navigator in my response to the acquisition? I asked
myself. "Probably" was my answer at the time. It still is
today at some level.

Out of my friend's questions came a very real sense
that I could do more for my team by doing more for
myself. Specifically, I needed to get my head and heart
around the acquisition and work hard to find and communicate the opportunity. Knowing that this wasn't going
to be easy, I asked one of my mentors for help. I received
a lot of good advice from my mentor, but one gem that
really stands out even today is the issue of the choices we
have when dealing with change. In hindsight, this may
have been the infancy of my whole thinking about our
workplace choices.

The net result of this is that we have choices in terms
of how we respond to the changes. There are of course
corresponding outcomes and even consequences to each
of the choices we make. As my mentor friend said, you
and your team can choose to ignore all of the directives
coming from corporate. This was obviously not a reasonable choice, but clearly it was a choice. After several
discussions about the choice issue it became clear how I
could help my team and myself respond more favorably
to the acquisition related "turbo" change.

We began to look at all of our choices related to every
aspect of the organizational change and also began to
weigh the impact of each choice option. This became
known among our team as the Cost-Benefit Analysis
drill. Very simply, this allowed us to identify the costs and
benefits of every one of our choice options. To make it
even more real in our world, we measured these costs and

benefits against key barometers like customers, organization and team. We would actually evaluate every choice scenario against these factors, and in a very short period of time we realized that the only viable choice was to take action and move forward in support of making the change work for everyone. To be sure, an outcome that only comes from navigating at a very high level.

Group Activities FOR BUILDING A NAVIGATOR CULTURE

1. Solicit feedback from your team relative to what they believe to be the forces of change in your department or organization. Establish ongoing dialogue with them to help identify how these forces of change will continue to shape their jobs in the future.

2. Review your score from the Change Management Leadership Inventory and identify two areas that you could work on to improve for the benefit of your team.

3. Explore the Leadership Communication strategy formula and identify what you could be doing more and less of to help create greater clarity for your team.

4. Initiate a discussion with your peer group about how the rumor mill impacts the realization of your business objectives. Also consider a review of the indirect role that leaders may play in feeding the rumor mill.

5. Incorporate a discussion of new workplace realities and associated expectations including key actions and behaviors in all staff meetings and look for ways to reinforce positive behavior and progress.

Chapter Six

LESSONS FROM THE NAVIGATOR'S NOTEBOOK

1. The first responsibility of a leader is to define reality.
2. Navigating is the only choice for leading your team through change.
3. Everybody goes through the change cycle in their own way and in their own time.
4. Eliminating the personal context of change allows folks to see the possibilities.
5. Every day presents an opportunity to be a role model for your team.
6. Clear, consistent and frequent communication greatly reduces the rumor mill.
7. Holding every person accountable is part of what good leaders do.
8. Using humor when appropriate may help more folks discover the silver lining.
9. Some people need more help than others to get on the bus.
10. Celebrating even small successes along the way helps.

The POWER of
COMMUNICATION

*"I was grateful to answer promptly, I
said I don't know" —Mark Twain*

"We're going to need to ratchet up our bandwidth, increase our throughput, and drill-down on our competencies to shore up our ROI following the RIF." What? you ask. This is not from a Dilbert cartoon, although it certainly could be. If you are like the client of mine and his twenty or so colleagues who actually heard this nonsense, your head might just be spinning by now. I know mine was following the call from this client who began the conversation with "I just heard the best one yet." I must admit, some days I don't have to look far for the humor in corporate life, and the day I received that call sure was one of those days. Ratchet up the bandwidth. Heck, this wasn't even an electronics manufacturer. It was a financial services company, and a large one at that.

Okay, enough of my poking fun at corporate life. Let me create a context. The above statement was made by a regional Vice President who had called a meeting of department managers to discuss a pending lay off. I think what she was really trying to say was something like,

"We're all going to need to work even harder following the layoff." How much easier and clearer was that? The truth of the matter is that simple communication seems to be less of the norm these days. It has been replaced by "corporate speak," a method of communication that seems to promote status over clarity. I have been more than a little bit amazed by what appears to be a correlation between the person's job level and the amount of "corporate speak" they spew, at least in the middle leadership ranks.

I have been in meetings where there was even an undercurrent of "corporate speak" competition at play. Managers of people vying for more control and status by one-upping their colleagues with the repetitive use of terms like robust, ratchet up, bandwidth and paradigm. Jargon-spewing zombies indeed.

Why we don't choose simplicity over the ambiguous jargon-infused corporate speak is a question for scholarly researchers. Whatever the reason, one does not need to be an academic to realize the inefficiency associated with corporate speak. Simply, it does not enhance clarity, it enhances ambiguity.

WATCH THE BORDERS?

In today's fast and furious business environment, leaders can not afford to waste time. Nor can they afford to allow ambiguity to derail or misdirect the efforts and activities of their teams. Striving for clarity is not just good leadership; it's good business, too. Ensuring that everyone is on the same page takes work for sure, but think of the alternative. Consider the following story.

It is reported that J. Edgar Hoover was once surprised to discover a rather dramatic increase in FBI activity along the Canadian and Mexican borders. When the FBI Director investigated, he found the problem. It turned out that a month or so earlier his secretary had asked him to review one of his memos she had just typed for him. She wanted him to correct any errors before she sent the memo to FBI field offices. When Hoover finished his edits, he observed that the margins of the note were much too wide. So he wrote, "watch the borders" at the bottom of the memo and gave it back to his secretary to fix and distribute. She logically assumed that Hoover's "watch the borders" comment related to some intelligence alert that he wanted distributed to his FBI border patrols.

While it is unlikely that a communication error of such magnitude would occur in corporate life today, the likelihood that our written and verbal communication is misinterpreted remains a very real obstacle to achieving our business objectives. Often what we say and what is heard is amazingly different. Not surprisingly, the risk and complexity associated with this reality is of course magnified by the number of people on your team.

Acknowledging that clear communication starts with you is an important first step in solving the communication puzzle. After all, you are the role model and standard bearer. Huge responsibilities for sure, but huge opportunities, too. Assessing your communication skills and capacity is a natural extension of both the huge responsibility and opportunity. The following Workplace Communication Effectiveness Inventory is a valuable resource and tool for helping to gauge your communication style and impact. It also provides a development framework that will allow you to expand your capacity and impact.

Like all development plans, it is highly recommended that you start small and work to build momentum. Selecting and acting on one or two development opportunities in a meaningful way is far more valuable than selecting five or six for the sake of quantity. Remember, quality does matter.

WORKPLACE COMMUNICATION EFFECTIVENESS INVENTORY

Answer the following questions regarding your workplace communication impact as honestly and objectively as possible. Circle the number on the rating scale that best represents you. Five indicates *most* like you while one is *least* like you.

When I am communicating with my team, co-workers and customers, I:

1. Am able to establish rapport quickly

    5   4   3   2   1
2. Demonstrate active listening skills

    5   4   3   2   1
3. Avoid making "snap" decisions about others

    5   4   3   2   1
4. Allow the person to state their concerns

    5   4   3   2   1
5. Am aware of, and sensitive to, other styles

    5   4   3   2   1
6. Know how I am perceived by others

    5   4   3   2   1
7. Can guide a conversation to a win-win outcome

    5   4   3   2   1

8. Look for opportunities to build trust

   5   4   3   2   1

9. Can read and respond to non-verbal messages

   5   4   3   2   1

10. Exceed my communication goals

   5   4   3   2   1

Total Score:

If you scored **40** or more, you are a master of workplace communication effectiveness. If you scored between **30** and **39**, you are well on your way to being a master of workplace communication but need to improve your understanding of the process. If you scored less than **30**, this is an important development opportunity for you. Try to become a student of the process and look for ways to build on your communication skills. *When we communicate effectively, we succeed.*

As mentioned, the Workplace Communication Effectiveness Inventory is a good barometer of your communication capacity and impact. Like any important leadership responsibility, your capacity to improve greatly influences your impact.

TELL THEM SOMETHING, PLEASE

Jim was a general manger of a medium sized consumer goods manufacturer that had seen the usual shift in business strategy caused by intense global competition. He was by most accounts a good leader who consistently produced strong bottom line results. As the market became saturated with foreign competition, Jim's business unit underwent some tough cost-cutting measures in an effort to survive. Folks who had been with the company for many years often commented that they had never seen so much change in such a short period. To make matters worse, much of the change was being directed not by Jim and his leadership team but by corporate finance, which was located in the UK. Some days, Jim would tell me that he didn't know whether he was coming or going. He, like most of the people at his division, was stressed and a bit overwhelmed.

My role in working with Jim and his leadership team involved helping them create a leadership communication strategy for managing the change and as a result minimize the potential burnout associated with the change. We made good progress quickly except for one major obstacle that almost derailed our efforts entirely. Jim didn't always know the whole story behind the corporate-driven changes. He just knew that he had to make them happen. This was part of the new corporate yardstick that he was being measured by almost daily. As the rate of change accelerated, employees seemed to ask more questions. This from my experience is always the case. And remember, absent clear and consistent communication from you and your leadership colleagues, they make it up. It's called the rumor mill.

Jim's frustration with the constant barrage of questions began to show. He didn't have all of the answers and in his words, "I would never let the team know that." He was convinced that as a leader, you can never let your people know that you *don't know*. His routine response to folks became so ridiculous that the rumor mill was close to becoming the true reality at Jim's division. He would say things like, "I'll have to get back to you on that one" (and he never did), or "no comment at this time," or my favorite, "this subject is on a need to know basis and you don't need to know" What kind of message did that one send? You don't count? You're a loser? A huge mistake in leadership judgment for sure.

I had many long and at times difficult discussions with Jim about his style of communication. The turning point for him (at least I think it was) was when I asked him to put himself in his team's shoes for a moment. You can do the same with how you communicate your story. Think about it, does your communication build clarity or does it create resentment and fear? Does it inspire your people or does it feed the rumor mill with more questions than answers? Your team deserves the truth. Granted, there are times when some things must remain confidential and certain people need to remain out of the loop, but giving it to your people straight is still the best policy. At a minimum, it is a leadership communication policy that builds clarity, confidence, and trust. It also represents how true Navigators communicate both in and out of work.

UNDERSTANDING DIFFERENT STYLES

The range of different communication styles add to the complexity of the leadership communication equation. How you communicate with one employee may not be as effective with others on your team. As a starting point, it helps to create a framework for exploring the various communication styles that are typically at play in today's workplace. Clearly there are many ways of defining or categorizing different styles. In an effort to keep it simple and manageable, I have drawn from the DISC assessment model, which was originally developed by William

Marston back in the 1920s. While the Myers Briggs Type Indicator (MBTI) has much application with style differences, I find that the DISC model has a much greater emphasis on workplace communication and offers tremendous insight into the communication blind spots that all people have.

Using the DISC foundation as a baseline is a good way to understand the different styles that encompass your team. The following is the DISC foundation, which includes the key descriptors for each style.

D – Dominant Descriptors:	*I – Influencing Descriptors:*
Demanding	Magnetic
Ambitious	Enthusiastic
Assertive	Persuasive
Competitive	Optimistic
Decisive	Sociable
Results driven	Talkative
Big picture view	Political
Confident	Inspiring
Fact oriented	People oriented
Usually extroverted	Usually extroverted
S – Steady Descriptors:	*C – Compliant Descriptors:*
Stable	Conventional
Passive	Conservative
Patient	Analytical
Deliberate	Evasive
Predictable	Systematic
Possessive	Cautious
Change resistant	Accurate
Low key	Neat
Process oriented	Data oriented
Usually introverted	Usually introverted

More than likely the above DISC foundation has given you enough insight to assess your team's DISC profile with a reasonable amount of accuracy. It is important to remember that everyone communicates differently and that by actively tuning into some of the subtle differences, you can quickly improve your communication impact.

The following is a good communication framework to follow that incorporates the DISC model and reflects some of the subtle and not-so-subtle differences in how people communicate.

When communicating with a person who is *ambitious, forceful, independent, decisive, and strong willed,* which are all **D** characteristics,

* Be clear and to the point
* Stick to business
* Be well prepared and organized
* Don't talk about things that are not relevant
* Don't make their decisions for them
* Provide them with options

When communicating with a person who is *enthusiastic, friendly, charming, demonstrative and sociable,* which are all **I** characteristics,

Start with the personal side, create a warm and friendly tone

* Don't rush into the business at hand
* Don't deal with a lot of details, put things in writing
* Ask feeling questions to draw out their opinions
* Always be sure they understand your expectations
* Don't try to control the conversation

When communicating with a person who is *patient,*

predictable, steady, modest and relaxed, which are all **S** characteristics,

* Start with a personal comment, break the ice
* Present your case in a gentle, nonthreatening way
* Don't force them to make quick decisions
* Ask "how" type questions to draw out their opinions
* Look for ways to demonstrate that you're listening
* Don't dominate the conversation

When communicating with a person who is *conservative, perfectionist, neat, analytical and conventional,* which are all **C** characteristics,

* Prepare your case in advance and be ready for challenges
* Stick to business, no small talk
* Be accurate and realistic
* Don't be casual or informal
* Always have supporting data
* Ask "why" type questions to draw out their opinion

Being clear on the best approach to your communication obviously encompasses more than style. It also involves a heightened awareness about how your communication is received along with the potential barriers it may create. Like the earlier example of the dreaded annual performance review in Chapter Four, your communication needs to be clear, specific, actionable, and timely.

FROM FEAR TO HOPE

I received the call from my friend Doug only two months after the merger took place. His company, a large national provider of business-to-business services had merged with a rival firm based in another part of the country. This was of course touted as a merger of equals with tremendous upside potential for increased market share and revenue growth.

From a pure business perspective, it all made sense. From a people perspective, it was frightening to say the least. This was after all a merger of equals and there were bound to be redundancies, which of course meant lay offs. Doug had been at the table with the other senior executives when the merger integration plans were discussed and agreed upon. Yes there would be layoffs, but folks would be treated fairly in terms of severance and job search assistance. That was the good news. The bad news is that most of the senior executives believed that the folks who stayed would see the opportunity and would be thrilled to be part of a bigger and certainly more successful organization. Sure there were some who viewed things this way, but like most merger scenarios, there were many who did not. I honestly believe that this is not so much a result of people being resistant to change as much as it is the inherent human need for clarity and purpose.

After several more months the neglected people side of merger integration became obvious. Despite the common belief among senior management that people were on board, they were not. In fact quite the opposite was true. People were feeling neglected and morale began to suffer. Fortunately, Doug had been part of two other mergers in his long and distinguished Human Resources career, and he knew what had to be done. He knew as a beginning point the senior team had to acknowledge that they could have done more to help people successfully navigate the new culture and its corresponding demands. He also knew that people needed to be heard, that they needed to have a voice. Doug and I held numerous meetings with different employee groups and it became clear that folks were in fact struggling with new workplace realities. To his credit, Doug was able to get the senior leadership team together to create a unified communication strategy that addressed many of the employee concerns and fears. In only three short months, the anxiety associated with the unknown was replaced with a feeling of community and confidence in the future. The absolute most significant driver of this outcome from my perspective was the clarity, consistency, and frequency of the senior leader's communication. In doing so they helped move the new organization in a direction where fear was replaced with hope.

Workplace communication can be easy, but more times than not, it's very complex. Communicating with staff, customers, peers, and other co-workers requires great care and planning. One of the most important elements of planning is seeking to be a good listener. Knowing your communication goals and desired outcomes remain a critical piece of the planning puzzle too. However, absent a strong desire and commitment to be an active listener, your communication goals and desired outcomes may not be achieved.

Understanding that most people want to feel heard more than they want you to agree with them is a good foundation for achieving your communication goals. It's ironic that many people complain about not being heard, yet they rarely take the time to listen to others.

Despite the many challenges of communicating effectively, good communication skills can be learned. The following are some suggestions for improving your leadership communication effectiveness.

1. Concentrate on what the other person is saying. *Put yourself in "their shoes."*

2. Don't take the other person's reactions personally. *Work to understand their concerns.*

3. Share responsibility for the communication. *Help find solutions.*

4. Look for common ground. *Resist the temptation to focus solely on differences.*

5. Keep filters and stereotypes in check. *Don't prejudge the person's intentions.*

6. Don't interrupt the person. *Let them paint the whole picture.*

7. Have patience. *Slowing down is key to active listening.*

8. Restate what you think you heard. *Strive for clarity.*

9. Don't offer advice unless you're asked. *Listening occurs with your ears, not your voice.*

10. Keep a positive mental focus. *Your goal is to create a win-win every time!*

From improving interpersonal relationships to achieving more win-win outcomes, the pursuit of successful communication is worth the effort. We each have an opportunity to increase our communication effectiveness and impact. While the skills required to achieve this goal can be learned, they do not occur without awareness, commitment and practice. When we communicate effectively, we succeed.

As the range and pace of change accelerate at work and the demands of doing "more with less" become a daily reality, improving the impact of your leadership communication may be the first step in turning old challenges into new opportunities.

.

Group Activities FOR BUILDING A NAVIGATOR CULTURE

1. Review several recent written communications to your team and seek input regarding peoples perception of the message. Did everyone get the same message?

2. Share the Workplace Communication Effectiveness Inventory with colleagues and team members and identify one or two group development opportunities.

3. Explore the communication style of your peer group. Does it consistently produce clarity and confidence? What is one thing that each of you can do ***more of*** and ***less of*** to increase your communication impact?

4. Seek input from your team relative to issues that need more clarification.

5. Seek feedback from a trusted friend or colleague about your communication blind spots.

Chapter Seven

LESSONS FROM THE NAVIGATOR'S NOTEBOOK

1. Clear communication starts with *you.*

2. Clarity and understanding must be key goals of all communications.

3. Often what you say and what is heard is different.

4. Jargon-filled "corporate speak" does not promote clarity.

5. There is a correlation between your capacity to improve and your impact.

6. Its okay to say you don't have all of the answers.

7. As the pace of change accelerates, employees need more information.

8. Your team deserves the truth.

9. Navigators work to build clarity, confidence and trust in all communications.

10. Increasing communication effectiveness involves awareness, commitment, and practice.

CHAPTER EIGHT

HARNESSING
TEAM SYNERGY

*"The only happy people I know are the
ones who are working well at something
they consider important" —Maslow*

I had struggled to put my finger on it or to actually define it for a very long time. What I did know was that many leaders I had spoken with believed that doing a once-a-year team-building event was all that was needed to keep the team fully engaged. What I didn't quite understand was why they never seemed to do anything to connect the annual events. There never seemed to be any "in-between activities" to help build off the momentum of each annual event. In fact, I came to believe that the concept of continuity and momentum was not even part of the equation. This has always been difficult for me, because absent clear linkage the leader's capacity to build on the event outcomes is very limited. From a bottom line, cost-benefit perspective, it's almost like throwing money away. Clearly a no-win scenario by any measure.

The important leadership discovery related to this is what I have come to call the *Synergy Myth*. Very simply, the synergy myth is the false sense of accomplishment or progress that leaders often get following many team-building activities. They do a half-day or full-day or even a two-day event, and magically all of the barriers to collaboration are supposed to be removed. They have harnessed the collective talent and synergy of the team in only a matter of hours. Not exactly. So often these activities are stand-alone events with little or no connection to a larger process for improving employee engagement and collaboration. In true check-it-off-the-list fashion, many leaders assume that by doing some mix of learning and social activity, teams work more effectively. They don't in most cases. Perhaps for a few days or weeks after the event but rarely for an extended or sustainable amount of time. Add to this the lack of follow-up and accountability related to the team-building event and unfortunately the synergy myth becomes reality. After all, if we don't measure it, it doesn't exist.

Harnessing the collective talent of your team is not just a great leadership opportunity but also a great driver of your success. Your ability to get them to do their best in concert toward a common goal is one of the most important responsibilities you will ever have as a leader. It can make the difference between average performance and superior performance for sure. Achieving the latter obviously takes more than the occasional team-building event. As a beginning point, it takes a deep awareness about your team and an even deeper commitment on your part to choose the Navigator path every step of the way.

HOLD THE PEPPERONI PLEASE!

"That *was* your team-building event" Jim said as a dozen

of his employees listened in disbelief. For nearly six months Jim's direct reports had told him stories about the lack of synergy among team members at their NJ location. There had been many changes in their department and like most organizations everyone was called upon to do more with less. The whole team was feeling burnt out and now more than a few people were beginning to speak up. Something had to be done to address the poor morale and lack of synergy among the team.

Despite a growing frustration among his team, Jim refused to believe that there were conflict and collaboration issues with his team. Finally, after repeated requests from his most senior team members, Jim decided that he would address the team-building issue. During one of his routine monthly visits to the NJ office, he announced that he was taking everyone out for pizza and beer after work. He went on to say that he had heard that folks were not working well together and that this type of social activity would be "just the thing they needed" to get along better.

While this type of activity is not a bad thing, no reasonable person can expect that it solves a conflict and collaboration issue that has festered for six months or longer. To make matters worse, Jim made his pizza and beer announcement just ninety minutes before the end of the work day. Even if people wanted to attend, it would be difficult given the very short notice. The net result, only 4 of the 27 members on Jim's NJ team showed up for pizza and beer. The remaining team members were left more frustrated and resentful by Jim's lack of leadership. In not digging deeper and being more mindful of the issues, Jim's pizza and beer team-building event did more harm than good.

Knowing that Jim's failed team-building attempt had

created even worse working conditions, one of Jim's team leaders made a point of talking about it on the weekly managers conference call. "That was a real missed opportunity," she said to Jim referring to the impromptu pizza and beer team-building event. "When are we going to do a real team-building event?" she asked. "That *was* your team-building event and nobody chose to come so you obviously don't have any issues," Jim replied. What a missed opportunity indeed.

Unfortunately the story doesn't end here. After repeated requests for some type of team intervention, Jim finally agreed to get the whole team together for a team-building event. His solution, a paint ball adventure where team members formed small groups who then hunted the other team members. I have heard of some pretty ridiculous team-building ideas in my career, but this one takes first prize. How shooting each other with a paint ball builds collaboration and trust is totally beyond me. Jim would have gotten far more out of the event if he simply let everyone shoot him with paint balls. At least then they would have been doing something in concert, toward a common goal.

BUILDING THE AWARENESS FOUNDATION

Like many teams today, your team is likely multi-tasking at a very high level. The white-water pace of your work environment rarely affords the opportunity to take extended periods of time away from the business at hand. Even a half-day away from the office can add many more hours to your team's individual and group workload. The truth is that because of your hectic work pace, *you can't afford not to take time out* for team development. The further away your folks get from a common ground or shared sense of community, the greater the potential for breakdowns in communication, collaboration, and teamwork.

Like many worthwhile leadership endeavors, harnessing the collective talent of your team requires that you build from a foundation. In this case, a very important building block of the foundation is linked to the team's shared values. In Chapter Four, "The Satisfaction Continuum," I briefly explained the shared values link to employee satisfaction.

The application in this chapter is more foundational in that you *explore* rather than define the shared values of the group. As you might imagine, only your team can really define their shared values. The best you can do as the leader is help guide them through the exploration process. That's not to say that your values shouldn't be part of the shared values. They should. To make it more meaningful the emphasis needs to be on the collective group and not any single member of the team.

One of the best ways to guide your team through the values-exploration process is to engage them in a discussion about your own values. If your team doesn't know what your values are, they are less likely to be open about their own values.

Several years ago I developed a very useful values related exercise for a client who at the time was the head of a medium-size IT group. The exercise, called the *Team Rules to Live By* exercise, provided this client with an effective process for guiding his team through the values exploration process. Since that time, I have modified the exercise several times, which has resulted in a still effective but more streamlined process. The following represents the key components and flow of the exercise, which has proven to be very valuable for many leaders and teams over the past six years.

TEAM RULES TO LIVE BY EXERCISE

Two Steps, Approximately 30 minutes

Step One: As part of a staff meeting or team-building event, have all team members list the three most important rules that they "live by" on either an index card or separate piece of paper. These rules that they live by can also be defined as their internal guideposts, their values, beliefs, convictions etc. A few of the examples that I have heard with some degree of frequency include: Measurer twice and cut once, Listen more and talk less, Respect for others, Family first, The Golden Rule, Integrity and Professionalism.

Once the team has created their list, the facilitator then charts all responses on a flip chart. Note, the success of the exercise has been increased by prefacing the whole exercise with a discussion about how values play out at work and how ultimately they help define who we are both as individuals and team members. Linking the exercise to you own personal experiences will of course increase the success of the exercise at an even high level.

Step Two: From the rules listed on the flip chart, team members are asked to identify the two or three rules that the *team should live by* to ensure collaboration and long-term success. Once the team has identified the top three rules to live by, everyone receives a printed copy of the rules, which they agree to post in their office or work area. Note, I have found it most effective when the team is split into groups of 4 to 6 for this portion of the exercise.

The net result of your thirty-minute investment in the above exercise is that your team will not only have greater clarity about their shared values but will likely have a renewed sense of team spirit and synergy too.

I have done the Team Rules To Live By exercise dozens of times and it has always produced a positive outcome. Placement of the exercise when it is part of a larger off-site event is an important consideration. In this scenario, I typically do the exercise toward the end of the event and in some cases at the very end as the final exercise. In a few cases, I have used it as the kick-off exercise in a two- or three-day conference where we want to set the collaboration tone early in the event. Like any worthwhile team development activity, the long-term impact and value needs to be driven by you the leader.

One of the best ways to drive the long-term impact is by always staying connected to the activity outcome. In the case of the team rules, it is helpful to present them as the guiding principles of team conduct for all interactions. Investing five minutes in every staff meeting to talk about how they apply to each team member is another good way to stay connected to the exercise outcome. It also helps to revisit the entire exercise once or twice a year to ensure that the rules are current and real for every member of your team. Finally, in case your team gets stuck with putting their own rules or values into words. I have listed below a values primer of sorts that helps folks get unstuck very quickly.

Family	Money	Friendship	Ethical
Integrity	Status	Creativity	Community
Professionalism	Power	Variety	Quality
Serving	Recognition	Independence	Solitude
Loyalty	Winning	Flexibility	Low Stress
Respect	Advancement	Balance	Security
Honor	Personal Success	Faith	Team Success

Remember, there are no wrong answers when it comes to personal values.

ADDING THE BRICKS & MORTAR

Another outcome of today's hectic work environment is the multitude of distractions that individuals and teams encounter. Competing agendas, knee jerk reactions of poor leadership, customer demands, poor communication etc. etc. All of these distract employees at some level. One of the most common byproducts of these daily distractions is that left unchecked, employees easily shift into the FM zone. They shrink with fear, anxiety and frustration all while moving potentially deeper into the detour behaviors.

Helping their teams see beyond the distractions is an important part of what great leaders do day in and day out. Helping them get reconnected to their successes and what they have to be proud of is a powerful way of guiding your team to see beyond the distractions.

In early 2001 I was working with a group president of a small manufacturing firm who knew all too well about his team's distractions. As he put it, "My team is so distracted by organizational change and all sorts of other related things that they just don't seem to have any gas left." He knew that they had an impressive history of doing good work and as a team had shared in many successes. We both thought long and hard about how we could get them reconnected to this history of success so that they could see beyond the many daily distractions at work. After numerous brainstorming sessions, we came up with a group exercise we called Discovering Our Strengths. It proved to be a very effective process for not only reconnecting his team to their proud history, but also giving them a renewed sense of hope for the future.

The group exercise, done as part of a larger team development off-site retreat, allowed the team to examine their successes at a level that included the key drivers of their success. It also helped to reconnect them to their core values.

The following represents the key components and flow of the exercise, which has worked very well with many teams over the past six years.

DISCOVERING OUR STRENGTHS EXERCISE

Four Steps, Approximately 60 minutes

Step One: Participants are asked to define

the 2 or 3 greatest wins of the past year. *Note*, these can be on any one of three levels: Organization, Department/Team or Individual. In small groups of 2 to 5 allow them 10 to 15 minutes to process this segment.

Step Two: Once the answers from Step One are charted, participants are asked to define the Success Characteristics that created these wins. These Success Characteristics are really the drivers of the success outcomes from above.

Step Three: With answers from the first two steps charted, participants are asked to identify the things that make them proud to be part of the team or organization.

Step Four: Debrief with emphasis on key learnings and the team's overall success capacity. Some helpful follow-up questions include; What does this tell us about our ability to handle change?–How are the Success Characteristics linked to our core values as a team? - How are the sources of pride linked to our core values as a team?–What can we do as a team to stay connected to our proud history of success? An important frame of reference when doing the debrief is to remind your team that the Wins are the *What* of their accomplishments, The Success Characteristics are the *How* of their accomplishments and the sources of Pride are the *Why* of their accomplishments.

The *Discovering Our Strengths* exercise has become one of my favorite team development exercises because it consistently produces many positive outcomes.

It has always resulted in a higher level of team synergy with every team and has served as a powerful reminder of what teams can do when they work together toward a common goal.

BUILDING LINKAGE

Helping your team to stay connected to any team development activity outcome does not have to be complex or time consuming. One of the best ways to create linkage is to include focused discussions related to the activity in periodic staff meetings. Even one twenty-minute discussion per month will allow your team to stay connected while building momentum toward the accomplishment of their shared goals.

Soliciting input directly from your team is another way to create linkage. So often, we allow our own leadership distractions to get in the way of finding bigger and better solutions for more than just the team synergy issue. You can bet that not only does your team have some good solutions for creating linkage, but they also would like to share them with you.

Just like helping your team to stay connected doesn't have to be complex or time consuming, the whole process for team development doesn't have to be either. Beyond acknowledging the need to do related activities more often than once a year, it helps to engage the resources of your Human Resources or Talent Management team. If by chance you don't have that function at your organization, don't despair. There are many external resources that can support your efforts with team development. In addition to local universities and professional associations that might offer assistance, there are numerous books on the subject. One of my favorites is *Quick Team Building Activities for Busy Managers* by Brian Miller (AMA Publishing). In it Brian offers over fifty team development activities that help leaders improve team collaboration, communication, problem-solving, and creativity. There are also numerous on-line resources that are available.

Regardless of which resource you tap, it helps to have a high degree of clarity around where you need the help in your team development efforts. The following is a team development survey I use in my consulting work that is designed to help build clarity for both my clients and myself.

TEAM DEVELOPMENT
NEEDS ASSESSMENT

1. What is the level of trust among the team?

2. How does the team handle conflict?

3. What is the level of participation among the team?

4. How does the team deal with change and ambiguity?

5. What motivates the team?

6. What is the level of leadership sophistication among the team?

7. What leadership gaps can you identify relative to this group?

8. How do these gaps impact the business unit?

9. What is the team's perception of this?

10. What is the CEO's perception of this?

11. What is the average tenure of this group?

12. What behaviors would you like to change?

13. What theme or principles need to be incorporated into the training event?

14. What are your desired outcomes?

15. How can we measure these outcomes?

16. How much planning time do we need?

17. What resources are available to help with the event?

18. How will the team respond to the event?

19. How does the event get communicated (positioned) and by whom?

20. What time commitment will I need to make for event follow-up?

Completing the Team Development survey is a good first step in planning for a meaningful team development activity or event. It also helps to be mindful of the time allotment for each segment or activity of the overall event. I remember getting a call from a colleague of mine not long ago who was deeply frustrated by her client's desire to do a strategic planning and team-building event in a half-day format. They expected to get a team of twenty senior leaders together who had a history of not working well together and were convinced that a half-day event would be just what they needed. It is hard enough to do a strategic planning activity in a single day, let alone a few hours. The whole point here is that quality always beats quantity, at least with team development and probably leadership too. Trying to harness the collective talent and synergy of your team only once a year or in a few short hours is a sure way to keep the *Synergy Myth* alive.

Exercises FOR BUILDING A NAVIGATOR CULTURE

1. Identify at least two follow-up actions that you can take to create linkage to your last team development activity or event.

2. Complete the Team Development Survey to help identify the top two barriers to team synergy and collaboration within your area. Develop a plan for addressing these development opportunities.

3. Incorporate the Team Rules To Live By exercise in your next staff meeting and seek input from your team on individual actions that will help create linkage to team success.

4. Include the Discovering Our Strengths exercise in your next team-building event and develop a plan to help monitor weekly or monthly successes.

5. Solicit input from your Human Resource or Organizational Development partners to explore team development resource options.

LESSONS FROM THE
NAVIGATOR'S NOTEBOOK

1. The synergy myth creates a false sense of progress.

2. Creating linkage between events builds momentum.

3. If you don't measure it, it doesn't exist.

4. Your success is tied to your ability to harness the collective talent and capacity of your team.

5. The white-water pace of today's business environment demands that you take time out for team development.

6. Only your team can define their shared values.

7. Your team's values should be the guiding principles of all interactions.

8. There are no wrong answers when it comes to personal values.

9. Left unchecked, daily distractions can shift employees into the FM zone.

10. Harnessing team synergy is not just a leadership obligation, it's an opportunity too.

NAVIGATING *as a* CAREER MANAGEMENT STRATEGY

"I always wanted to be somebody; I just should have been more specific" —Groucho Marx

We had just landed a major contract with a local division of a global aerospace leader, and we were energized to say the least. This was the sweet fruit of our very long and at times intense collaborative efforts. My team and I were chosen to help develop an internal career management training program for upwards of 2,000 people. In true Navigator fashion, we all embraced the opportunity. Beyond providing project management support, I was entrusted to write the first few modules of the training program. One of my big challenges as my client described it was to set the *personal accountability/opportunity* tone in the first few pages of the workbook. She went on to say that she wanted employees to understand *their role* in the career-management process as well as the opportunity that was being presented by the company. She wanted them to see the opportunity and seize it quickly. Her boss, the divisional president, summed up this expectation and reality another way. "We'll provide them with the car, but they have to drive." He equated all of the many internal

development resources to nothing short of a huge investment for every employee, "kind of like buying each of
them a car" he went on to say.

I had my usual intense workload at the time and
frankly struggled a bit with the magnitude of my task.
As if this was not enough, one of my team members
reminded me that the success of the program at an
important level would be linked to my ability to get folks
engaged quickly. No small task for sure. I went about my
writing and followed the usual format that has worked
well for me over the years. I began with the end in mind
and proceeded to work my way back to the beginning, all
while searching deep for some pearls of wisdom that in
this case would ignite personal accountability early and
often.

One day when I was driving to an appointment, the
thought occurred to me that personal accountability was
really about ownership. Owning your success I believe
drives personal accountability. I also believe that personal
accountability is a critical part of career management. At
last, I had it, *Career Ownership, the belief that I am the chief
architect and sculptor of my work experience and career success.*
This was all about "driving the car," I thought. It also has
a lot to do with navigating I later discovered.

The "driving the car" analogy really resonated with
me. I immediately envisioned career management from
the passenger seat perspective. Allowing someone else
to drive the car on my career journey didn't make sense
then and it sure doesn't make sense now. Yet all of us
including myself have done it from time to time. In doing
so we become dependent on the other person's ability to
take us where we want to go. Even worse, we sometimes
allow the other person to set the course for us. The net

result is the dependency factor, which for me at the time was the missing link in my training module writing challenge. If Career Ownership is the belief that I am the chief architect and sculptor of my career success and satisfaction, then *Career Dependency is the belief that some one else is responsible for my career success and satisfaction.* Someone else drives the car.

EXPLORING THE NAVIGATOR-PERSONAL ACCOUNTABILITY LINK

Despite the fact that the Career Ownership–Career Dependency discovery occurred nearly fifteen years ago, I only recently began to understand its link to the four behaviors. Sure there are some obvious parallels to navigating, but there are also some very strong links to the detour behaviors.

One of the common denominators that the victims, critics, and bystanders share is the absence of personal accountability, especially at work. Like with the Career Dependency choice, these behavior choices hold others accountable or at least responsible for their circumstances. Always choosing to point the finger at some one else if things aren't going their way. How convenient, they're not happy with the destination so they naturally blame the boss or whoever else was driving their career car. This is another great example of how they relinquish their power when they choose the detour behavior path.

Like most leaders today, you probably struggle with the personal accountability issue within your team or across your organization. Even a minimal increase in personal accountability can produce significant improvements in productivity and morale. I know because I've helped tackle this issue with more than a few leaders and organizations.

As a beginning point, I have found it helpful to get team members engaged in helping to define what personal accountability means in their world. To be sure, there are differences among some groups, but overall there are many similar characteristics and behaviors that support personal accountability. The following is a summary of what I have discovered about these characteristics and behaviors in my coaching and training assignments over the past seven years.

PERSONAL ACCOUNTABILITY
Characteristics:

Integrity, Self-awareness and control, Commitment, Adaptability, Dedication, Business acumen, Initiative, Confidence, Courage, Objectivity, Results oriented, Collaborative, Career Ownership.

PERSONAL ACCOUNTABILITY
Actions & Behaviors:

1. Accepts responsibility for own decisions and performance.

2. Displays confidence in decisions and commitments, even under pressure.

3. Is proactive and demonstrates initiative in honoring commitments.

4. Expresses ideas and expectations clearly and confidently.

5. Appropriately challenges 'status quo" firmly and diplomatically.

6. Owns one's actions, behaviors and success.

7. Sets realistic goals and expectations.

8. Demonstrates energy and persistence in tackling challenging assignments.

9. Consistently meets or exceeds team and customer expectations.

10. Takes responsibility for own progress and seeks continuous improvement.

An important leadership consideration in nearly every one of my group or individual conversations about personal accountability is that leaders must demonstrate a higher level of personal accountability because they need to inspire and motivate personal accountability within their teams. A tall order for sure, but one that is not difficult when you choose career ownership on the Navigator path.

Much of what Career Ownership encompasses is about a career management strategy with its all important personal accountability driver at the very root of the equation. At an even deeper level, navigating encompasses a mind set and an internal operating system where the career management strategy resides. After all, the strategy is only one dimensional in that it is a single piece of a larger process or methodology for creating work and life success.

Career management is all about creating options. This alone is a good motivator for most people. Being clear about what goes into a career management plan is very important. Absent a high degree of clarity around what you need to be doing to support your plan is key. It also helps to be able to gauge your own level of career readiness before you begin a new plan or even modify an existing plan. The following Career Readiness Profile is a helpful tool for doing just that. It is designed to provide you with some meaningful insight into many of the important aspects of a proactive career management plan.

CAREER READINESS PROFILE

Answer the following questions regarding your career management effectiveness as honestly and objectively as possible. Circle the number on the rating scale that best represents you. Five indicates *most* like you while one is *least* like you.

When I think about my career management, I:

1.   Am clear about my top three work related values

    5   4   3   2   1

2.   Have a well defined set of career goals for next year

    5   4   3   2   1

3.   Understand what my manager expects of me

    5   4   3   2   1

4.   Can identify at least one development opportunity

    5   4   3   2   1

5.   Am aware of the top three trends impacting my job

    5   4   3   2   1

6.   Can identify one opportunity to expand my value

    5   4   3   2   1

7.   Can easily identify my key strengths

    5   4   3   2   1

8.   Know how I am perceived by others

	5	4	3	2	1
9.	Can name three people who will support my goals				
	5	4	3	2	1
10.	Have a meaningful plan for achieving my goals				
	5	4	3	2	1

Total Score:

If you scored **40** or more, you are a master of career management effectiveness. If you scored between **30** and **39**, you are well on your way to reaping the rewards of a proactive career management plan. If you scored between **20** and **29**, this is an important development opportunity for you. Try to become a student of the process and look for ways to increase your effectiveness. A score of **19** or less means that the health of your career is in jeopardy. Identify the statements that you scored lowest on and develop a plan to accomplish these critical steps in the career management process. *Effective career management is all about options!*

While all of the above statements represent important parts of a proactive career management plan, some are more critical than others. At a very high level on the importance scale is what your manager or board of directors expects of you. Absent total clarity, you can't possibly hit the mark with any degree of consistency. I have been amazed over the years by the number of leaders, even very senior leaders, that I've spoken with who can't tell me in absolute terms what their managers expect of them. There are the rather obvious but sometimes nebulous items like increased shareholder value and improved return on investment. Important measures for certain, but hardly enough to paint a clear picture of what the key stakeholder of your job expects.

In addition to being clear on stakeholder expectations, it helps to be clear on the scope of resources that are available to help you meet those expectations. It is also important to consider how all of this has changed or evolved and how it will likely evolve in the future. Clarity around all of these issues helps to eliminate the guess work, which obviously is not an option when you're navigating at any level.

In response to these important issues and of course the larger issue of personal accountability, I created a three-part exercise that I call Role & Resource Clarity. I have used it with teams and with many coaching clients with a high degree of success. Following are the three segments of the exercise.

R O L E   &   R E S O U R C E C L A R I T Y   E X E R C I S E

Key Questions

Segment One:

* What are the five most important responsibilities of your role?
* What are the key resources for getting the job done?
* What skills, talents, and attitudes are required for achieving success?

Segment Two:

* Who are the three most significant stakeholders of your work?

* What are the two most significant expectations of each stakeholder?
* How can you build more clarity around stakeholder expectations?

Segment Three:

* How has your role evolved in the past twelve months?
* What changes can you identify relative to new demands and expectations?
* What steps can be taken to better meet current and future expectations?

As you can see, these questions do not allow for quick or simple answers. They are not intended to be easy questions. Like any worthwhile endeavor, what you get out of it has a lot to do with what you put into it. I encourage you to explore each and every one of the above questions more than once a year and certainly over more than one day. In building clarity around these important issues, you are not only demonstrating personal accountability and career ownership but also navigating at a high level.

THE 5% FORMULA

My decision to dedicate this book to my dad was easy. Beyond being a great father, he was the most decent and selfless person I've ever met. We never got to talk about my four behaviors theory, but I know if we had, he would certainly be able to relate. Everything he did was about taking the high road. He was a Master Navigator for sure. He was also a deeply religious and principled man.

He didn't say much, but when he did it was always kind, respectful, and meaningful.

Earlier in my career and shortly after my second promotion to the leadership ranks, I remember asking my dad about his leadership success formula. He had enjoyed a distinguished forty-year career in law enforcement and had retired as one of the most senior members of his agency. He was a highly successful and well-respected professional by all accounts. His answer to my success formula inquiry was quite powerful in its simplicity. He was quick to say that a lot of things had influenced his success over the years, but one thing that stood out for him was his 5% Formula.

His 5% formula, he went on to tell me, was about always giving 5% more than people expect. He had worked with a lot of people over four decades and had certainly observed a wide range of successful people over that timeframe. He said he was lucky to learn this early in his career, and as a result made this one of his important guideposts along the way. He went on to say that it had been his observation over much of his career that very few people actually give 100% of themselves to their work. In fact, he didn't think that giving 100% was realistic. "The best you can do is exceed their expectations," he said. Sometimes that takes 80% of your effort and other times it takes 90% of your effort, but it always takes 5% more than they expect. My dad's 5% Formula has played a very real and beneficial role in my career and life success since that father-son conversation twenty years ago. Giving 5% more than is expected in any area of your life, be it work or family or friends, goes a long way in a creating a higher level of success and satisfaction. It also represents a powerful example for your team as you lead them to the Navigator path.

EXPLORING THE CAREER
ACTION INVENTORY

One way to lead your team to the Navigator path is to help them understand the broader context of career management. While it is important to have a plan that reflects role and resource clarity, this is simply not enough. As a leader, you have a wonderful opportunity to guide each member of your team on their own development journey. Sure they have to drive the car, but you must play a supporting role, much like a co-pilot or navigation officer. Without your guidance, they might just get to the wrong destination, which obviously serves no one's best interest.

The following Career Action Inventory is a very useful tool for examining the broader context of career management. It provides an excellent framework for building or expanding a career management plan.

THE CAREER ACTION INVENTORY
Your Road map to Career Ownership

The Career Action Inventory and Planning Guide is designed to help you examine and map a variety of issues and factors that affect your career. This guide will help establish an important frame of reference as you navigate your work life. As your world of work evolves and new skills are required, your ability to thrive *versus* survive will ultimately determine the range of options available to you. It is with this outcome in mind that the following information is presented.

Many factors form, shape, and even guide the choices we make about our careers. As such, the framework of the Career Action Inventory & Planning Guide encompasses four critical issues that must be considered to ensure a high level of impact and success. *Self, Profession, Organization,* and *Industry* are all part of the larger range of issues and factors that affect your career today and certainly well into the future.

Remember, there are no wrong answers to any of these questions. Additionally, don't expect to have all of the answers today. Like any worthwhile endeavor, your outcomes will be tied to the time and energy you invest.

INVENTORY SEGMENT

Self: Gaining clarity around the "you" of the career management equation.

1. My three most important work-related values are:

2. My three most valuable work-related skills are:

3. The three areas of my work that I excel at include:

4. What do you enjoy most about your work?

5. If you could replace 20% of your job with something different, what would it be?

6. Why would you make this choice?

7. How would people you work with describe you? What is your reputation?

8. What is your best or biggest development opportunity right now?

9. What benefit would you receive if you seized this opportunity?

10. What do you want most from your career?

11. What are your career goals for the next two or three years?

12. What obstacles might get in your way? What solutions can you identify?

Profession: Gaining clarity around external factors.

1. What are the three most relevant trends impacting your profession?

2. What skills will be required in the future to be considered an expert in your field?

3. What do you need to do within the next year to maintain your competitive edge?

4. Which professional organizations are most beneficial to your development?

5. Who are the five people you consider to be experts in your profession?

6. What professional organization offers the most valuable networking opportunities?

7. What association meeting can you attend in the next 60 days that will best support your career management goals?

Organization: Gaining clarity around internal factors.

1. What are the three most significant trends impacting your organization?

2. How will your job be different one year from now? Three years from now?

3. What are the core competencies that will be required of you in the future?

4. How will our customers change over the next few years?

5. What are the key strengths of your organization? Your function?

6. Who are the key stakeholders of your job?

7. Who are the people in your organization that can become your career sponsors?

Industry: Gaining clarity around more external forces.

1. What are the three most significant trends impacting your industry?

2. What opportunities are associated with these trends? Personal? Business?

3. Who will the top three market leaders be in your industry two years from now?

4. What competencies will be most rewarded in the future?

5. What can you do to respond to the changes in your industry?

Planning Guide

1. I can do the following to respond to my inventory results:

2. The most important step I will take toward greater career ownership is:

3. I will take this action not later than:

4. The three most important resources to help me achieve my goals are:

5. I'll know I'm on the right track when:

6. The three people who can/will support my efforts are:

7. The professional organizations I need to belong to are:

8. The one professional development action I will take within 30 days is:

9. The three most relevant competencies I will build on *or* acquire are:

10. The cost of not having a career action plan is:

Notes to myself:

_____

_____

_____

_____

_____

_____

Leading your team to the Navigator path takes more than a detailed career management plan. But this is certainly a good step in the right direction. Helping your team to view the plan as a work in progress is also a step in the right direction. So often employees get overwhelmed by what they perceive as the complexity of a meaningful career management plan. Worse yet, they perceive it as a no-win situation because they don't have the benefit of a co-pilot or at least a manager who helps create clear and reasonable development goals.

Very few people I've spoken with over the last twenty or so years could tell you that they wake up every day with a clearly defined career management strategy. I know I can't. I'm sure that many of your employees couldn't either. That's all okay. I have found in both my own experience and in many client experiences that you don't need to have a daily career management road map to be successful. Rather, what you need is a desire to have more options and a willingness to hold yourself account-able for your own success. In embracing the career ownership concept, we all have an opportunity to not only design the road map but also drive the car.

Activities FOR BUILDING A NAVIGATOR CULTURE

1. Engage your team in a discussion about the Career Ownership and Career Dependency concept. Ask them to define what this means to them and also ask them to identify the key actions and behaviors that foster career ownership.

2. Explore the personal accountability issue with your peer group to assess how well you demonstrate the appropriate behaviors. Consider having each peer identify one thing they can do **more of** and one thing they can do **less of** to help foster personal accountability.

3. Review the Career Readiness Profile and identify at least one development opportunity related to your own career management strategy. Ask your team to do the same.

4. Incorporate a discussion about the Role and Resource Clarity exercise in your next staff meeting and ask all team members to complete the exercise as part of their own career management plan.

5. Ask all team members to complete the Career Action Inventory and incorporate a 10 to 15 minute discussion about the inventory in every staff meeting for the next 6 to 12 months.

Chapter Nine

LESSONS FROM THE
NAVIGATOR'S NOTEBOOK

1. Career Ownership is all about driving the car.

2. The driver's seat is always a better choice.

3. Career Dependency relinquishes your power.

4. Even a minimal increase in personal accountability is powerful.

5. Leaders must demonstrate a higher level of personal accountability.

6. Career management is all about increasing your options.

7. Options are good.

8. Absent total clarity you can't hit the mark every time.

9. Without your guidance your team may arrive at the wrong destination.

10. Giving 5% more of yourself in any area of your life is a good formula for Navigating.

LEADING CHANGE
FROM *the* TOP DOWN

A Case for Executive Sponsorship

MAJOR FOCUS OF THE CASE

Few leaders have been trained how to lead and implement change. This case is about a CEO who learned how to lead change the hard way. His first effort at making a major change in his company failed. When the persistence of the Human Resources Senior Vice President finally got his attention, he took a totally different approach to organizational change and saw much better results. The case provides many valuable lessons on leading organizational change.

DAN'S FIRST APPROACH TO
MUCH NEEDED CHANGE

Noble Insurance (NI) like many US based life insurance providers was beginning to feel the effects of the economic downturn in Q1 2005. For the first time in its proud 42 year history, NI failed to meet revenue goals for the previous year. Despite the fact that earnings had been off for the two previous quarters, Dan Arnold, NI's Chairman and CEO did little to act on this until early 2005. With concern growing among his executive team, Dan decided that it was time to act. With minimal input from his Board or senior team, Dan announced that all departments in the company were to reduce operating expenses by 20% effective immediately. In addition to cost cutting measures, department heads were expected to eliminate any open positions and were told to be prepared for staff reductions in the future.

Within the first three months following Dan's cost cutting mandate, employee morale had sunk to an all time low. Not surprisingly, a decline in productivity followed. Even the most well intentioned and motivated employees were beginning to feel the stress that resulted from the cost savings initiative. People were being asked to do considerably more with less and despite the efforts of some leaders; most people were completely unaware of what was behind this new and painful direction. Ambiguity led to fear which in turn led to a very distorted rumor mill at the company.

By the time Kim Jeng, NI's SVP of HR got involved, several of the top employees had left to join competitors. Citing input and concern from her staff around the country, Kim informed Dan that the pace of change and resulting ambiguity had become a major barrier to organizational success. She went on to say that if NI didn't act soon, the long term viability of the company might be in jeopardy. As a long time, trusted member of Dan's team, her feedback got Dan's attention.

Despite Kim's good work in developing an organizational response strategy, Dan refused to be part of the process. He went on to say that this was a *people issue* and that people issues were best handled by HR. He was also quick to say that due to the demands placed on other executives, that this new change management initiative should be driven by mid level managers under the direction of HR.

THE HR EXECUTIVE'S EFFORTS TO INFLUENCE NEEDED CHANGES

In early Q3 2005 Kim and her team had selected an external resource for helping to implement and manage the change management project. It was determined that all managers would go through a full day of change management training and that all employees would attend a similar ½ day workshop. Following all of the training which took three months to deliver, the change management vendor met with Kim and her team to review progress and to make recommendations for the future. At first glance, the project appeared to be a success. Nearly 75% of all leaders and 82% of employees had attended the training. Dan was pleased with seeing this project come to a close. It was one more initiative to check-off his list. *Things were sure to be better now* he thought.

While the change management training did produce some benefits, it was widely perceived as a *band-aide* approach. Many of the leaders who did attend the training commented in private that they felt isolated from the big picture issues that were driving change in the first place. They also expressed a sense of resentment for Dan and his executive team for their lack of participation and support. Some managers actually went as far as to sabotage employee attendance by not allowing employees to attend the ½ day sessions under the guise that scheduling was too cumbersome and complicated.

As the beginning of 2006 rolled around employee morale at NI had declined to a point where nearly all employees began to have serious doubts about the future of the organization. Despite some communication clarity and consistency from field office middle managers, the rumor mill was in high gear across the organization. Most of the rumor mill exchange focused on *how good* things used to be and *how terrible* things had become at NI. Not surprisingly, Kim and her team of dedicated HR professionals began to notice a huge spike in Employee Relations cases. The daily average of employee sick days per department also spiked to an all time high.

A PROACTIVE AND PERSISTENT HR EXECUTIVE FINALLY REACHES THE CEO

Frustrated and deeply concerned about the future of NI, Kim decided that it was time to get Dan involved in more than an ancillary role. She and her team began to research *best practice* approaches to organizational change and workplace resilience. After nearly two months of research, she was convinced that Dan had to lead the change charge. In her meeting with Dan, Kim explained that she was still proud to be part of NI but that she felt very strongly that Dan needed to play a much more active role in helping the organization to move forward. She went on to say that all of her research pointed to the critical need for the CEO to not only drive the change initiative but also to embrace it as a long term process.

Kim's dedication and impressive record of accomplishments over the previous 18 years at NI helped in getting Dan to consider her recommendations. He admitted to Kim that he also sensed that NI was not the great company that it had been in years past. Almost sheepishly, he went on to say that he felt responsible for allowing NI to get to this point. He too wanted to believe in the future of NI and was now prepared to do his part in getting the organization back on track.

THE CEO'S NEW APPROACH
TO LEADING CHANGE

The first action that Dan took was to assemble his executive team for a long overdue conversation about NI's current state. He was surprised to learn from Kavi Jete, NI's General Counsel that most of the executive team shared in Kim's frustration and concern. Like most organizations their size, they all had been more than a little bit busy and distracted by the day to day demands of their functional areas. After listening to Kavi Jete and other members of his executive team for nearly two hours, Dan acknowledged that he was ready to lead the charge.

Recognizing that the current level of employee morale and reduced productivity were major barriers to success, Dan decided to seek input from employees across the organization. He wanted to know what was on their minds and what they needed from him and other leaders to help return NI to greatness. Unlike the first failed attempt at workplace resilience, Dan decided that he would lead this initiative. Within only three weeks, Dan personally visited all six of NI's locations. Through the help of Kim and her HR team, Dan was able to speak with nearly 80% of all employees through informal breakfast and lunch group meetings. At first, many of the employees were skeptical. After all, Dan had not been to most of these locations in over 2 years and many remembered his lack of involvement in the last change management initiative. Even more than this, they remembered his almost random cost cutting mandate that had produced such ill will across the organization. Sensing this wide spread skepticism, Dan admitted to the employees that he had not done a very good job last time around and that he had decided to take full responsibility for allowing NI to get to this point. He also informed them that they would be seeing a lot more of him and his executive team because now, they were all going to be responsible for helping NI to get back on track. Dan went on to say that they needed everyone's help and that this would be no small undertaking but that together, they would make NI a great place to work at once again.

Dan and Kim were both a bit surprised by the consistency of the feedback from employees across the organization. Sure there were those who were still very negative, but the vast majority of employees wanted to believe in a brighter future based in no small part on their proud past. With very little exception, the top three things that employees wanted answers to included, *what is happening? - why is it happening?* and *what do you expect from us?*

Realizing the importance of a consistent leadership response to these three critical questions, Dan and Kim decided to start with the executive team. Dan personally contacted each member of his executive team to discuss the employee feedback and instructed them to consider the three key questions. Within two weeks, Dan and his team met to discuss their communication strategy relative to the three key questions. The group quickly agreed that the sequence of questions made sense and that it was in everyone's best interest to keep things simple and clear. Like some executive teams, Dan and his team had been known to allow hubris to distort and dilute some executive communications in the past.

With the help of Kim Jeng as the facilitator, the executive team was able to agree to a real and meaningful response to each of the three key questions. They agreed that *what was happening* was that NI, like most insurance providers was being impacted by many external forces of change like; competition, demographics, regulations, technology and the overall state of the economy. After considering each of these external change factors, the group was able to see that these factors not only represented *what was happening* but also *why it was happening*. Finally, the group agreed that what was expected of each employee was no different from what the executive team expected of each other, to act with integrity and purpose, to stay positive and hopeful and to remember that we're all in this together and that when one of us succeeds, we all succeed.

While Dan was very pleased with the outcome of the executive team meeting, Kim expressed some caution. She went on to say that while this was a very powerful message, it might not reflect the thinking of the broader leadership across NI. After all, the many front line mangers that would need to carry the message across NI should have some input on what was being communicated relative to the three key questions. Dan agreed with Kim's assessment and instructed her to set up a series of meetings with leaders across the organization. Over the next four weeks, Dan and Kim held eight communication strategy meetings with all leaders across NI.

The reaction from most leaders including many other employees was very positive. This was the second time that Dan had visited their location in under a year and once again, he was looking for their input. In each of the leadership communication strategy meetings, Dan shared what came out of the executive team communication strategy session. He indicated that he thought that it was a good start but that he was sure it could be improved upon by leadership groups across NI.

While there were some varying opinions on the overall content of what was being communicated relative to change at NI, Dan and Kim were able to build clarity and consensus across the leadership ranks at NI. By using the three key questions as framework, the leadership team now had a clear and consistent story to tell about organizational change and transformation at NI.

Not content to leave leadership communication to chance, Dan asked all leaders to develop a proactive process for sharing the new leadership communication across the organization. As a beginning point, they agreed that Dan would do a company-wide communication once per month to update employees on NI's progress and also to seek input from employees about what leaders could be doing to help them succeed. It was agreed that Dan's first monthly communication would include the leadership team's answers to the three critical questions as well as lessons learned to-date.

One of the many important lessons that Dan and his executive team learned through the process was that some employees need more help than others to navigate organizational change. To this end, Dan enlisted the help of Kim and her HR team to offer change specific training across NI. He also initiated a monthly leadership conference call to update leaders on financial performance and to allow all leaders to share lessons and successes relative to the organizational transformation. Not surprisingly, this monthly exchange of leadership thinking went a long way in building further clarity and consistency around leadership communications.

Dan and his executive team worked diligently over the next two years to be role models for change by being more visible and engaged in the change process. The monthly conference calls and employee updates from Dan served to create many important outcomes including improved morale, collaboration, clarity and purpose.

THE RESULTS OF EFFECTIVELY LEADING NEEDED CHANGE

Today, nearly six years after Dan's ill fated cost cutting mandate, NI is enjoying double digit growth and employees have a renewed sense of hope in the future. Dan continues to do his monthly conference call for leaders and is now doing a quarterly employee communication that includes performance data, leadership strategy and updates on the three critical questions related to organizational change and transformation.

TEAM DISCUSSION SUGGESTIONS:

1. Evaluate the CEO's initial approach to change in 2004-2005 and the consequences of this approach.

2. As a leader leading change, how could the CEO have approached the need for change differently?

3. As a potential change champion yourself, what can be learned from the way the HR SVP finally got the attention of the CEO?

4. Discuss why it is important for leaders to have a leadership style that welcomes open communication and feedback and the correlation between leadership communication and employee morale.

5. What did the CEO do to lead change the right way the second time and what different outcomes were achieved?

6. Are there other things the CEO could have done to more effectively lead the change process the second time?

7. What value does leadership transparency play in reducing the rumor mill?

8. Why is executive sponsorship critical?

KEY LEADERSHIP LESSONS:

1. Organizational change and transformation is a continuous process not an event.

2. Organizational change is most often driven by external factors.

3. As the pace of change accelerates, employees want and need more information.

4. Absent clarity and consistency from the leadership team, employees feed the rumor mill

5. Most employees want to believe in the organization and its future.

6. Executive sponsorship of organizational change and transformation is critical.

7. Everyone responds to change differently and some employees need more help than others.

8. Every leader is a role model for the organization.

CHOOSING *the* NAVIGATOR'S PATH

"opportunityisnowhere"

Whether you saw "opportunity is now here" *or* "opportunity is no where," you're right. The power of your perception and associated beliefs will almost always drive your attitude and ultimately your behavior. Our ability to grasp this and even explore this reality in our world is, I believe, an important step in being able to spend more time on the Navigator path. Of course it's not as simple as this. As mentioned in Chapter Two, most days it takes work, lots of work, to challenge and then shift from the detour behavior perception to the Navigator or AM screen. Some days the shift to the Navigator path seems entirely too hard and out of my reach. Other days find me waking up almost mysteriously in the AM zone. I will admit that those days are not, for me anyway, the norm.

Over the past six years I have had many conversations with friends and business colleagues about the human capacity to shift to the AM screen and as a result end up spending more time on the Navigator path. Regrettably, I have yet to discover a magic formula that allows for instant, on-demand shifting. I have, however, developed and even honed some techniques that over time seem to allow me and others to spend less time in the FM zone operating within the toxic boundaries of the detour thinking and behavioral choices.

I have talked about or referenced the internal guidepost concept at many points in this book. At the very center of this internal source of wisdom and perspective lie our core values. These are the guiding principles that define who we are and how we operate. They are the truths that we have discovered on our journey and hopefully that allow us to have a higher purpose along the way. As I look back on my journey since the sabbatical, I honestly believe that those times when I had the greatest amount of values clarity was also when I navigated more frequently. Values clarity for me really means that I am not only clear about what my values are, but also clear on the actions in my daily life that allow me to live and honor these values. Sure there are distractions along the way, but staying connected to your core values allows you to tap your internal guidepost with greater ease. It also allows you to navigate more often.

PRACTICE WHAT YOU PREACH

Maria was a mid-level manager who like most forty-something professionals was overworked and a bit stressed. One day on her way to work she realized that she had forgotten about an important meeting that she was to attend for her boss. At about that point, she also realized that the meeting was in fifteen minutes and that she was at least twenty minutes away from the office. Frustrated and certainly a bit more stressed, she approached the next major intersection and found herself second in line at the traffic light, which had just turned red. Anxious, she began to tap on the steering wheel and repeatedly looked at her watch. As the light turned green, the one car in front of her stalled. Maria grew even more frustrated and anxious. Just as the light turned yellow, the driver in front of her re-started the car and darted through the yellow light, leaving Maria at the red light for a second time.

By now, Maria was ready to scream. She was surely going to be late for the meeting, she thought. Again she tapped the steering wheel and anxiously looked at her watch. She was going to make it through the intersection *this time*, she thought. Just as the light turned green, a school bus pulled into the intersection from the other direction and proceeded to signal the flashing red lights of a pick-up or drop-off. No children appeared to be entering or exiting the bus.

Maria became furious. She began to blow the horn and shout at the bus driver. When this didn't seem to work, she rolled down her window and began to scream at the bus driver. A few obscenities could be heard coming from her car. Just as Maria thought that the bus was about to move, a loud pounding noise came from the back of her car. In a split second, a police officer appeared at her car window and proceeded to physically remove her from the car. She was shocked and overwhelmed to say the least. Without notice, the police officer placed her in handcuffs and put her in the back of his police cruiser.

Maria became hysterical. A police supervisor was called to the scene in an effort to get her to calm down. Not only was she going to miss the meeting, she was sitting handcuffed in the back of a police car. After a few minutes, the police supervisor took Maria from the cruiser and removed her handcuffs. He went on to explain that the first police officer had been right behind her at the traffic light and that he had observed her irrational behavior. More importantly, he said, the officer noticed the many bumper stickers on her car that proclaimed things like *Serenity Now, Practice Random Acts of Kindness,* and *Patience Is a Virtue.* Seeing these, the first officer was convinced that the car was stolen as the behavior of the driver was completely opposite of the bumper sticker messages.

What do your work- and life-related "bumper stickers" say about you? Can people tell your values by your actions? How often do you put out mixed or even contradictory messages about your values? Great leaders never do. They operate from a level of clarity and values-driven purpose that allow them to walk the talk every day. This is powerful for sure. It is part of the power that every one of us posses if we choose to believe in our power and our voice. Sure, it's easy to forget, to be distracted and even fearful of our power. Nelson Mandela in his 1994 inaugural speech said among other things that, "Our deepest fear is not that we are inadequate. Our deepest fear is that we are powerful beyond measure. It is our light, not our darkness, that most frightens us."

You are powerful. The person sitting next to you is powerful. The co-worker who you don't necessarily like is powerful. Acknowledging and recognizing our power and the power of others can only come from the AM zone. In the FM zone we feed the fear. We shrink and discover all kinds of reasons to not believe in our power. We give up our power when we're in the FM zone. We surrender our power when we choose the victim or critic path. Think about it, being a victim is feeling and believing that you're powerless. Victims in any realm rarely feel powerful. The exception may be the power that comes from the "misery loves company bus" scenario which produces some level of status and hierarchy along the way. Remember, some victims and critics wear these behavior labels as badges of honor.

NO SPACE FOR RENT

Guarding our AM zone is another way to harness the power that allows us to stay on the navigator path. A long time ago in a job far away, I had a series of bad bosses who in hindsight were likely put on my path for good reason. Of course at the time I didn't see it this way, but now I do. They were all there to teach me about bad leadership and to stretch my capacity to be a good leader.

In my final year with that company, I had the worst boss ever. He was an intense, very insecure, and controlling-type manager who was just plain mean. My colleagues and I used to wonder how he ever got hired and even more importantly how he continued to get promoted. It was not a fun experience by any means.

Fortunately for me he was transferred to corporate headquarters after only three months. Unfortunately, he remained my boss. We would need to speak at least once per week and sometimes more often. The pattern that quickly developed on these calls was ugly and toxic. He would go out of his way to belittle me and my team and was never happy with our results, even though they were consistently positive. He seemed to get great pleasure out of making me feel inferior, which by the way he did quite well. After most calls I would retreat to the parking lot of my building and just walk around until I regained my composure. I was struggling with this, and it wasn't getting better or easier.

You can be sure that I shared my frustration with many colleagues but never my staff. I knew that they saw my boss as a monster, and I was determined to do everything possible to shield them from his toxic behavior. One day I ran into a dear friend that I had not seen in a very long time and I shared my story about the phone calls from my boss. His first response was, *"Why are you letting him rent space in your head for free."* I must admit that I was more than a little curious about what this meant. He was also quick to say that I needed to *"take back my power."* He went on to say that I was giving this person too much power in part by letting him into my head so much, and that in doing so I was relinquishing my own power. How often do we all do this? How often do we let negative, toxic people rent space in our heads for free? If you're like me, the answer is probably too often.

While all of this made sense, I still hadn't connected all of the dots, so to speak. I still needed a mechanism to connect the dots and specifically a method for applying this new truth. I knew for sure that I was letting my boss rent space in my head for free, and I also knew that I was giving him way too much power. How could I take back my power?

I needed something that reminded me of my power and certainly of my options for handling these intense phone calls. For a very long time I have had good results with using different types of association techniques that allowed me to stay connected to a particular truth or lesson. The blue marble from Chapter Two is a great example of how I have used and continue to use association techniques to stay grounded. Unfortunately for me, this whole toxic boss experience was many years before I received the blue marble.

Ironically, what I did use for my association technique with the toxic boss was also blue.

I had just finished a series of workshops where we
used colored stickers and dots to illustrate a key learning
point. I had sheets of these colored dots left over and they
would stare me in the face every time I opened my top
right desk drawer at work. One day it all came together.
The blue dot (I had more of these than the other colors)
would be my association technique. I would put it on my
phone and whenever my boss called it would remind me
of my power and my options for dealing with him in a
more effective, less stressful way. I was open to anything at
that point and I figured that this was worth a try. Early on
it felt awkward, but after a few months it became hugely
successful. So much so that I actually felt good about getting the calls. I had my power back, and not surprisingly
my relationship with the toxic boss improved.

There are many association techniques that you can
use to produce a similar outcome in your world. The first
step is to of course acknowledge your own power. You
have immense power. Focus on your power and huge
capacity to bring your own goodness and light to every
interaction, to every experience you have. Maybe it's a
blue dot or marble, maybe it's a piece of art work in your
office, maybe even a photograph on your desk. It can be
anything. The critical point is to be able to link all of
your power and capacity for goodness to the object. In
my case with the blue dot on my phone, that represented
and reminded me of my power and goodness every time
I looked at it. It allowed me to stay connected to the AM
zone, and as a result have a wider range of options for
dealing with toxic people and their detour behaviors. It
takes time, but believe me, it's worth the effort. I have

many association links in my life today all of which are connected to my desire to navigate at a high level both in and out of the space I call work.

Staying connected to the AM zone is from my experience the most direct path to navigating. Appreciating our gifts, talents and blessings allows us to shift from the detour behavioral choice and related FM zone to the Navigator path with greater speed and ease. Gratitude is a powerful prescription for being able to spend more time on the Navigator path.

Out of genuine gratitude comes a quiet confidence that says I'm okay and that my power is about good energy and staying true to my values. How many times do we allow the FM zone to dictate our reality and the way we act or respond to key people in our lives? The answer for most of us is too much or too often.

Choosing the Navigator path is also about examining our expectations and how they play out and often distract us in our FM zone. Rarely do our expectations distract us when we're in the Appreciation Mode because out of gratitude we're able to shift our focus away from expectations. So often we want more or expect more than what we have or where we find ourselves along the journey. I remember a time in my life many years ago when a dear friend of mine seemed very distracted by all of the things that she didn't seem to have in her life. By her estimation her life was empty, a series of one failure after another. Wanting to help, I asked her one time what she thought was behind these almost debilitating feelings. She was quick to reply that she wasn't happy with where she was in her career and life and that she felt a constant hunger or search for something more. I don't know where the following questions came from, but I do know that I felt them very strongly. "*What if you could know today with absolute certainty that this was the best your life would ever be?*" and "*How would that knowing change your view point?*" I asked.

Imagine that for a moment. You are exactly where you are supposed to be right now. Your life is exactly where it is supposed to be right now too. Are these tough questions to ponder? You bet they are. They're real and even painful for some folks but not the Navigator. Navigators trust that they are on the right path. They know that by living their values they are always moving in the right direction. They also know that life throws curve balls some times but at the end of the day, they are exactly where they are supposed to be. Their values and internal guideposts tell them so.

Staying true to your values and helping your team do the same is a huge responsibility of good leadership. It is also one of the great opportunities associated with good leadership. Just as you and I get distracted in the FM zone, your team does too. Helping your team move beyond the FM and into the AM takes work, but it's not overly difficult if you work to understand their distractions. Often one of the biggest distractions in today's work environment is workplace stress. Stress comes from all sorts of things: expectations, new demands, internal politics, conflict, detour behaviors, and certainly organizational change. Developing mechanisms to combat workplace stress is an important step in helping your team to get unstuck from the FM zone. It is also an important step in choosing the Navigator's path.

FINDING YOUR STRESS
COMFORT ZONE

Everyone needs a certain amount of stress to function. Obviously, some folks do a better job dealing with stress than others. Finding your stress comfort zone is a good place to begin in the process of managing workplace stress effectively. Your stress comfort zone is the range that allows you to function effectively and stay healthy. It's the place that you become painfully aware of when you're approaching its outer limits. I recall a story I used to tell in my stress management classes that illustrates the stress comfort zone quite well.

When my daughter was just beginning first grade, my wife had a very demanding job that often required her to be in the office at 7:00 a.m. Because I was self-employed, the school transportation duties became part of my morning routine. Anyone who has ever had a five-year-old will most certainly relate to the following scenario. Most mornings found me watching the clock with a great deal of intensity. After all, despite the fact that I was self-employed, I still had a job and all of the usual demands that went with it. I knew for example exactly what had to be accomplished in our morning routine within various time frames. By 6:45 a.m. she should have had breakfast and been fully dressed for school. By 7:00 a.m. I needed to have her lunch made and packed. Between 7:05 and 7:15 a.m. we needed to be out the door. Most mornings the routine went well. Some mornings it did not.

A favorite ploy of my daughter's was to announce that she didn't like her outfit just as we stepped outside to enter the car. In hindsight, I think Murphy's Law was working against me because this typically happened on the mornings when we had surpassed our 7:15 a.m. departure goal. My mind would begin to race, *what route will have the least traffic, how can I make up the time, should I let her change?* Often the answer to the last question was a big no. Even the no answer required extra time because at age five you're programmed to challenge every no answer. I would find myself rationalizing why she didn't need to change or why her outfit looked just great. Some mornings I would just give in and let her change. Despite the fact that this would only add 5 or 10 minutes to our routine, I could feel myself approaching the outer limits of my stress comfort zone. Only minutes earlier I was in the AM zone of being a grateful and proud father and now I was late. Not a good experience for either of us.

As I approached the outer limits of my stress comfort zone, I could feel myself quickly shifting into a place where I was angry, resentful, and just plain stressed. All because my expectations and plans weren't working. I am embarrassed to say that some mornings when this happened I would be so far out of my stress comfort zone that I would play the "parent card." "I'm the boss, the answer is no, get over it, get your butt in the car," all of which got both of us more stressed. Over time and with a lot of reflection and practice, I got better at dealing with this scenario. Taking a step back and putting things in perspective often allows us to stay within the boundaries of our stress comfort zone, which ultimately affords us the opportunity to stay more connected to the Navigator path.

Finding and exploring your stress comfort zone also allows you to stay more grounded. Being grounded, or centered as some people call it, is another direct path to Navigating.

At an even deeper level I believe is what I like to refer to as harmony. The concept of harmony goes beyond values alignment and even being grounded. It is by my estimate a more holistic view and reality that is well worth striving for on our journey.

My exploration of the harmony concept really stems from the many great leaders that I've worked for or with and even the many that I have interviewed over the last dozen or so years. There are of course many things that stand-out among great leaders, and it has been my humble attempt to capture many of them in this book. One of the characteristics that has really stood out with these leaders is that they navigate at a very high level both in and out of work. There seems to be a perfect alignment and deep connection between who they are in both realms. I think that this may just be one of the highest levels of Navigating. Harmony, work and life aligned. A great place to be for sure.

I am certain that the harmony concept is available to all of us. I am also certain that it doesn't just happen but rather takes commitment, personal reflection, persistence, and a lot of motivation.

My motivation for choosing the Navigator path has a lot to do with the fact that Navigating allows me to be much more of the person that I want to be and I know am capable of being in all aspects of my life. Knowing that bad leadership produces far more victims and critics is another motivation. Whatever your motivation is for choosing the Navigator path, I'm sure you'll agree that the world needs far more Navigators and far fewer victims and critics. Great leadership is about consciously choosing the Navigator path at every juncture, every day. When we let our own light shine, we unconsciously give other people permission to do the same.

Group Activities FOR BUILDING A NAVIGATOR CULTURE

1. Share the opportunityisnowhere statement with your team and explore how individual perceptions influence the behaviors of the team.

2. Initiate a discussion with your team and peer group about the techniques that they have used to successfully manage workplace stress.

3. Do an inventory of what your "bumper stickers" say about who you are. Do your actions support and reinforce the message of who you are? Ask your team to do the same.

4. Who are the toxic people that rent space in your head for free? How can you take back your power?

5. Solicit input from your team and peer group about the top three to five "team motivators" for choosing the Navigator path.

Chapter Eleven

LESSONS FROM THE
NAVIGATOR'S NOTEBOOK

---

1. Our perception is our reality.

2. We surrender our power when we take the victim path.

3. Clarity of values is a good path to more frequent Navigating.

4. Acknowledging our own power is another path to Navigating.

5. Gratitude is a powerful prescription for being able to spend more time on the Navigator path.

6. Navigators trust that they're always on the right path moving in the right direction.

7. Taking a step back and putting things in perspective often allows us to stay within our stress comfort zone.

8. Harmony is available to all of us.

9. Dysfunctional, ego-driven leadership creates more victims and critics.

10. Honoring our core values and voice keeps us on the Navigator path.

SHARING *the* GIFT

When I first set out to write this book, I wasn't entirely sure what direction the book would take. I certainly had some ideas and of course started with a chapter sequence draft but still wasn't certain where it would lead me. What I was very sure about was my overall motivation for wanting to write the book. In some small way, I wanted to share my own lessons about leadership with the hope that in doing so more people would discover their capacity to lead with grace and conviction both in and out of work. After spending four years of my life writing this book, that motivation remains the driving force behind this book *and* my consulting work.

It has been my observation over the past twenty years that dysfunctional leaders extinguish the hope and power of their employees. In doing so, they create legions of victims and critics who readily surrender their power and light in the name of survival. There is a better way, and it begins with you. You have the capacity to honor not only the power and light of your employees but also your own light.

The world we live in is hungry for good leadership. Every day we are given the opportunity as leaders to honor and nurture the people that we are called to lead. This is by my estimation one of the greatest gifts of the leadership path. Helping your team discover their own path to navigating is the ultimate gift of leadership. Sharing this gift is more than a leadership responsibility; it is an obligation that must be fulfilled. In being open to tapping your own internal guidepost as you fulfill *your* obligation, you automatically give your team permission to do the same.

INDEX

ABOUT *the* AUTHOR

 David A. O'Brien is President of Work-Choice Solutions, a trusted provider of leadership and team effectiveness consulting services that was founded in 2000. Prior to WorkChoice Solutions, David was a Senior Vice President & General Manager with a global provider of workforce management services. His Organizational Development consulting career spans twenty five years and includes key leadership and P&L responsibility within a variety of industries including, Manufacturing, Healthcare and Financial Services.

In his current role, David is responsible for providing leadership and team effectiveness training, coaching and consulting services to organizations throughout the United States. His clients include such market leaders as Aetna, Allied World, Avery Dennison, ConnectiCare, Dow Chemical, ESPN, KPMG, MetLife, Otis Elevator, PeoplesBank, The Hartford, Travelers and United Technologies. He also works with many small and emerging market leaders as well as a wide range of non-profit clients to help bring about sustainable improvements in organizational effectiveness.

To learn more about the scope of David's work in helping leaders and teams to maximize their performance potential or to arrange for David to speak at your next conference, please visit WorkChoice Solutions on line at: www.workchoicesolutions.com or call David directly @ 860.242.1070.

The Navigator's Compass:
101 Steps Toward Leadership Excellence

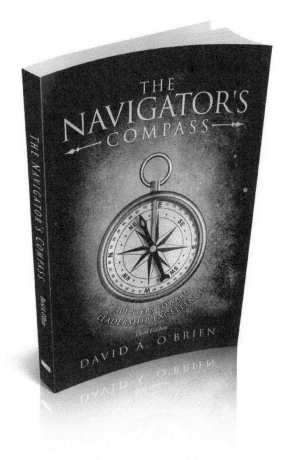

To get your copy visit
www.DavidOnAmazon.com

Made in USA - North Chelmsford, MA

10.12.2020 2036